D0880252

THE RED BOOK
OF
GUERRILLA WARFARE

By

Mao Zedong

El Paso Norte Press
Special Edition Books

The Red Book of Guerrilla Warfare
By Mao Zedong

Edited by Shawn Conners

Copyright © 2010 by El Paso Norte Press

Translation of "On Guerrilla Warfare" by Samuel B. Griffith in Fleet Marine Force Reference Publication (FMFRP) 12-18, 1989

Additional translation by Foreign Language Press, Peking

First Edition – January 2010

Published by
El Paso Norte Press
El Paso, Texas USA

ISBN10 1-934255-27-0
ISBN13 978-1-934255-27-8

Printed in the United States of America

CONTENTS

THE RED BOOK
OF
GUERRILLA WARFARE

Part 2:
Problems of Strategy in Guerrilla War against Japan

Mao Zedong

THE RED BOOK
OF
GUERRILLA WARFARE

PART 1

ON GUERRILLA WARFARE

Mao Zedong

CHAPTER I

What Is Guerrilla Warfare?

In a war of revolutionary character, guerrilla operations are a necessary part. This is particularly true in war waged for the emancipation of a people who inhabit a vast nation. China is such a nation, a nation whose techniques are undeveloped and whose communications are poor. She finds herself confronted with a strong and victorious Japanese imperialism. Under these circumstances, the development of the type of guerrilla warfare characterized by the quality of mass is both necessary and natural. This warfare must be developed to an unprecedented degree and it must co-ordinate with the operations of our regular armies. If we fail to do this, we will find it difficult to defeat the enemy.

These guerrilla operations must not be considered as an independent form of warfare. They are but one step in the total war, one aspect of the revolutionary struggle. They are the inevitable result of the clash between oppressor and oppressed, when the latter reach the limits of their endurance. In our case, these hostilities began at a time when the people were unable to endure any more from the Japanese imperialists. Lenin, in *People and Revolution* said: "*A people's insurrection and a people's revolution are not only natural but inevitable.*" We consider guerrilla operations as but one aspect of our total or mass war because they, lacking the quality of independence, are of themselves incapable of providing a solution to the struggle.

Guerrilla warfare has qualities and objectives peculiar to itself. It is a weapon that a nation inferior in arms and military equipment may employ against a more powerful aggressor nation. When the invader pierces deep into the heart of the weaker country and occupies her territory in a cruel and oppressive manner, there is no doubt that conditions of terrain, climate, and society in general offer obstacles to his progress and may be used to advantage by those who oppose him. In guerrilla warfare we turn these advantages to the purpose of resisting and defeating the enemy.

During the progress of hostilities, guerrillas gradually develop into orthodox forces that operate in conjunction with other units of the regular army. Thus the regularly organized troops, those guerrillas who have attained that status, and those who have not reached that level of development combine to form the military power of a national revolutionary war. There can be no doubt that the ultimate result of this will be victory.

Both in its development and in its method of application, guerrilla warfare has certain distinctive characteristics. We first will discuss the relationship of guerrilla warfare to national policy. Because ours is the resistance of a semi colonial country against imperialism, our hostilities must have a clearly defined political goal and firmly established political responsibilities. Our basic policy is the creation of a national united anti-Japanese front. This policy we pursue in order to gain our political goal, which is the complete emancipation of the Chinese people. There are certain fundamental steps necessary in the realization of this policy, to wit:

1. Arousing and organizing the people.
2. Achieving internal unification politically.
3. Establishing bases.
4. Equipping forces.
5. Recovering national strength.

Mao Zedong

6. Destroying enemy's national strength.
7. Regaining lost territories.

There is no reason to consider guerrilla warfare separately from national policy. On the contrary, it must be organized and conducted in complete accord with national anti-Japanese policy. It is only those who misinterpret guerrilla action who say, as does Jen Ch'i Shan, "*The question of guerrilla hostilities is purely a military matter and not a political one.*" Those who maintain this simple point of view have lost sight of the political goal and the political effects of guerrilla action. Such a simple point of view will cause the people to lose confidence and will result in our defeat.

What is the relationship of guerrilla warfare to the people? Without a political goal, guerrilla warfare must fail, as it must, if its political objectives do not coincide with the aspirations of the people and their sympathy, co-operation, and assistance cannot be gained. The essence of guerrilla warfare is thus revolutionary in character. On the other hand, in a war of counter-revolutionary nature, there is no place for guerrilla hostilities. Because guerrilla warfare basically derives from the masses and is supported by them, it can neither exist nor flourish if it separates itself from their sympathies and co-operation. There are those who do not comprehend guerrilla action, and who therefore do not understand the distinguishing qualities of a people's guerrilla war, who say: 'Only regular troops can carry on guerrilla operations.' There are others who, because they do not believe in the ultimate success of guerilla action, mistakenly say: 'Guerrilla warfare is an insignificant and highly specialized type of operation in which there is no place for the masses of the people' (Jen Ch'i Shan). Then there are those who ridicule the masses and undermine resistance by wildly asserting that the people have no understanding of the war of resistance (Yeh Ch'ing, for one). The moment that this war of resistance dissociates itself from the masses of the people is the precise moment that it dissociates itself from hope of ultimate victory over the Japanese.

What is the organization for guerrilla warfare? Though all guerrilla bands that spring from the masses of the people suffer from lack of organization at the time of their formation, they all have in common a basic quality that makes organization possible. All guerrilla units must have political and military leadership. This is true regardless of the source or size of such units. Such units may originate locally, in the masses of the people; they may be formed from an admixture of regular troops with groups of the people, or they may consist of regular army units intact. And mere quantity does not affect this matter. Such units may consist of a squad of a few men, a battalion of several hundred men, or a regiment of several thousand men.

All these must have leaders who are unyielding in their policies—resolute, loyal, sincere, and robust. These men must be well-educated in revolutionary technique, self confident, able to establish severe discipline, and able to cope with counter-propaganda. In short, these leaders must be models for the people. As the war progresses, such leaders lack of discipline which at first will gradually overcome the lack of discipline which at first prevails; they will establish discipline in their forces, strengthening them and increasing their combat efficiency. Thus eventual victory will be attained.

Unorganized guerrilla warfare cannot contribute to victory and those who attack the movement as a combination of banditry and anarchism do not understand the nature of guerrilla action. They say, 'This movement is a haven for disappointed militarists, vagabonds, and bandits' (Jen Ch'i Shan), hoping thus to bring the movement into disrepute. We do not deny that there are corrupt guerrillas, nor that there are people who under the guise of guerrillas indulge in unlawful activities. Neither do we deny that the movement has at the present time symptoms of a lack of organization, symptoms that might indeed be serious were we to judge guerrilla warfare solely by the corrupt and temporary phenomena we have mentioned. We should study the corrupt phenomena and attempt to eradicate them in order to encourage guerilla warfare, and to increase its military efficiency. 'This is hard work, there is no help for it, and the problem cannot be solved immediately. The whole people must try to reform themselves during the course of the war. We must educate them and reform them in the light of past experience. *"Evil does not exist in guerrilla warfare but only in the unorganized and undisciplined activities that are anarchism,"* said Lenin.

What is basic guerrilla strategy? Guerrilla strategy must be based primarily on alertness, mobility, and attack. It must be adjusted to the enemy situation, the terrain, the existing lines of communication, the relative strengths, the weather and the situation of the people.

In guerrilla warfare, select the tactic of seeming to come from the east and attacking from the west; avoid the solid, attack the hollow; attack; withdraw; deliver a lightning blow, seek a lightning decision. When guerrillas engage a stronger enemy, they withdraw when he advances; harass him when he stops; strike him when he is weary; pursue him when he withdraws. In guerilla strategy, the enemy's rear, flanks, and other vulnerable spots are his vital points, and there he must be harassed, attacked, dispersed, exhausted and annihilated. Only in this way can guerrillas carry out their mission of independent guerrilla action and coordination with the effort of the regular armies. But, in spite of the most complete preparation, there can be no victory if mistakes are made in the matter of command. Guerilla warfare based on the principles we have mentioned and carried out over a vast extent of territory in which communications are inconvenient will contribute tremendously towards ultimate defeat of the Japanese and consequent emancipation of the Chinese people.

A careful distinction must be made between two types of guerrilla warfare. The fact that revolutionary guerrilla warfare is based on the masses of the people does not in itself mean that the organization of guerrilla units is impossible in a war of counter-revolutionary character. As examples of the former type we may cite Red guerilla hostilities during the Russian Revolution; those of the Reds China; of the Abyssinians against the Italians for the past three years; those of the last seven years in Manchuria, and the vast anti-Japanese guerrilla war that is carried on in China today. All these struggles have been carried on in the interest of the whole people or the greater part of them; all had a broad basis in the national manpower and all have been in accord with the laws of historical development. They have existed and will continue to exist, flourish, and develop as long as they are not contrary to national policy.

The second type of guerrilla warfare directly contradicts the law of historical development. Of this type, we may cite the examples furnished by the White Russian guerrilla units organized by Denikin and Kolchak; those organized by the Japanese; those organized by the Italians in Abyssinia; those supported by the puppet governments in Manchuria and Mongolia, and those that will be organized here by Chinese traitors. All such have oppressed the masses and have been contrary to the true interests of the people. They must be firmly opposed. They are easy to destroy because they lack a broad foundation in the people.

If we fail to differentiate between the two types of guerrilla hostilities mentioned, it is likely that we will exaggerate their effect when applied by an invader. We might arrive at the conclusion that 'the invader can organize guerrilla units from among the people'. Such a conclusion might well diminish our confidence in guerrilla warfare. As far as this matter is concerned, we have but to remember the historical experience of revolutionary struggles.

Further, we must distinguish general revolutionary wars from those of a purely 'class' type. In the former case, the whole people of a nation, without regard to class or party, carry on a guerrilla struggle that is an instrument of the national policy. Its basis is, therefore, much broader than is the basis of a struggle of class type. Of a general guerrilla war, it has been said: 'When a nation is invaded, the people become sympathetic to one another and all aid in organizing guerrilla units. In civil war, no matter to what extent guerrillas are developed, they do not produce the same results as when they are formed to resist an invasion by foreigners. The one strong feature of guerrilla warfare in a civil struggle is its quality of internal purity. One class may be easily united and perhaps fight with great effect, whereas in a national revolutionary war, guerrilla units are faced with the problem of internal unification of different class groups. This necessitates the use of propaganda. Both types of guerrilla war are, however, similar in that they both employ the same military methods.

National guerrilla warfare, though historically of the same consistency, has employed varying implements as times, peoples, and conditions differ. The guerrilla aspects of the Opium War, those of the fighting in Manchuria since the Mukden incident, and those employed in China today are all slightly different. The guerrilla warfare conducted by the Moroccans against the French and the Spanish was not exactly similar to that which we conduct today in China. These differences express the characteristics of different peoples in different periods. Although there is a general similarity in the quality of all these struggles, there are dissimilarities in form. This fact we must recognize. Clausewitz wrote, in *On War*: 'Wars in every period have independent forms and independent conditions, and, therefore, every period must have its independent theory of war.' Lenin, in *On Guerrilla Warfare* said: 'As regards the form of fighting, it is unconditionally requisite that history be investigated in order to discover the conditions of environment, the state of economic progress and the political ideas that obtained, the national characteristics, customs, and degree of civilization.' Again: 'It is necessary to be completely unsympathetic to abstract formulas and rules and to study with sympathy the conditions of the actual fighting, for these will change in accordance with the political and economic situations and the realization of the people's aspirations. These progressive changes in conditions create new methods.'

If, in today's struggle, we fail to apply the historical truths of revolutionary guerrilla war, we will fall into the error of believing with T'ou Hsi Sheng that under the impact of Japan's mechanized army, 'the guerrilla unit has lost its historical function'. Jen Ch'i Shan writes: 'In olden days guerrilla warfare was part of regular strategy but there is almost no chance that it can be applied today.' These opinions are harmful. If we do not make an estimate of the characteristics peculiar to our anti-Japanese guerrilla war, but insist on applying to it mechanical formulas derived from past history, we are making the mistake of placing our hostilities in the same category as all other national guerrilla struggles. If we hold this view, we will simply be beating our heads against a stone wall and we will be unable to profit from guerrilla hostilities.

To summarize: What is the guerrilla war of resistance against Japan? It is one aspect of the entire war, which, although alone incapable of producing the decision, attacks the enemy in every quarter, diminishes the extent of area under his control, increases our national strength, and assists our regular armies. It is one of the strategic instruments used to inflict defeat on our enemy. It is the one pure expression of anti-Japanese policy, that is to say, it is military strength organized by the active people and inseparable from them. It is a powerful special weapon with which we resist the Japanese and without which we cannot defeat them.

CHAPTER 2

The Relation of Guerrilla Hostilities to Regular Operations

The general features of orthodox hostilities, that is, the war of position and the war of movement, differ fundamentally from guerrilla warfare. There are other readily apparent differences such as those in organization, armament, equipment supply, tactics, command; in conception of the terms 'front' and 'rear'; in the matter of military responsibilities.

When considered from the point of view of total numbers, guerrilla units are many, as individual combat units, they may vary in size from the smallest, of several score or several hundred men, to the battalion or the regiment, of several thousand. This is not the case in regularly organized units. A primary feature of guerrilla operations is their dependence upon the people themselves to organize battalions and other units. As a result of this, organization depends largely upon local circumstances. In the case of guerrilla groups, the standard of equipment is of a low order and they must depend for their sustenance primarily upon what the locality affords.

The strategy of guerrilla warfare is manifestly unlike that employed in orthodox operations, as the basic tactic of the former is constant activity and movement. There is in guerrilla warfare no such thing as a decisive battle; there is nothing comparable to the fixed, passive defense that characterizes orthodox war. In guerrilla warfare, the transformation of a moving situation into a positional defensive situation never arises. The general features of reconnaissance, partial deployment, general deployment, and development of the attack that are usual in mobile warfare are not common in guerrilla war.

There are differences also in the matter of leadership and command. In guerrilla warfare, small units acting independently play the principal role and there must be no excessive interference with their activities. In orthodox warfare particularly in a moving situation, a certain degree of initiative is accorded subordinates, but in principle, command is centralized. This is done because all units and all supporting arms in all districts must co-ordinate to the highest degree. In the case of guerrilla warfare, this is not only undesirable but impossible. Only adjacent guerrilla units can coordinate their activities to any degree. Strategically, their activities can be roughly correlated with those of the regular forces, and tactically, they must co-operate with adjacent units of the regular army. But there are no strictures on the extent of guerrilla activity nor is it primarily characterized by the quality of co-operation of many units.

When we discuss the terms 'front' and 'rear' it must be remembered, that while guerrillas do have bases, their primary field of activity is in the enemy's rear areas. They themselves have no rear. Because an orthodox army has rear installations (except in some special cases as during the 10,000-mile Long march of the Red Army or as in the case of certain units operating in Shansi Province), it cannot operate as guerrillas can.

As to the matter of military responsibilities, those of the guerrillas are to exterminate small forces of the enemy; to harass and weaken large forces; to attack enemy lines of communications; to establish bases capable of supporting independent operations in the enemy's rear, to force the enemy to disperse his strength; and to co-ordinate all these activities with those of the regular armies on distant battle fronts.

From the foregoing summary of differences that exist between guerrilla warfare and orthodox warfare, it can be seen that it is improper to compare the two. Further distinction must be made in order to clarify this matter. While the Eighth Route Army is a regular army, its North China campaign is essentially guerrilla in nature, for it operates in enemy's rear. On occasion, however, Eighth Route Army commanders have concentrated powerful forces to strike an enemy in motion and the characteristics of orthodox mobile warfare were evident in the battle at P'ing Hsing Kuan and in other engagements.

On the other hand, after the fall of Feng Ling Tu, the operations of Central Shansi, and Suiyuan, troops were more guerrilla than orthodox in nature. In this connection the precise character of Generalissimo Chiang's instructions to the effect that independent brigades would carry out guerrilla operations should be recalled. In spite of such temporary activities these orthodox units retained their identity and after the fall of Feng Line Tu, they were not only able to fight along orthodox lines but often found it necessary to do so. This is an example of the fact that orthodox armies may, due to changes in the situation, temporarily function as guerrillas.

Likewise, guerrilla units formed from the people may gradually develop into regular units and, when operating as such, employ the tactics of orthodox mobile war. While these units function as guerrillas, they may be compared to innumerable gnats, which, by biting a giant both in front and in rear, ultimately exhaust him. They make themselves as unendurable as a group of cruel and hateful devils, and as they grow and attain gigantic proportions, they will find that their victim is not only exhausted but practically perishing. It is for this very reason that our guerrilla activities are a source of constant mental worry to Imperial Japan.

While it is improper to confuse orthodox with guerrilla operations, it is equally improper to consider that there is a chasm between the two. While differences do exist, similarities appear under certain conditions and this fact must be appreciated if we wish to establish clearly the relationship between the two. If we consider both types of warfare as a single subject, or if we confuse guerrilla warfare with the mobile operations of orthodox war, we fall into this error: We exaggerate the function of guerrillas and minimize that of the regular armies. If we agree with Chang Tso Hua, who says - 'Guerrilla warfare is the primary war strategy of a people seeking to emancipate itself,' or with Kao Kang, who believes that 'Guerrilla strategy is the only strategy possible for oppressed people', we are exaggerating the importance of guerrilla hostilities. What these zealous friends I have just quoted do not realize is this: If we do not fit guerrilla operations into their proper niche, we cannot promote them realistically. Then, not only would those who oppose take advantage of our varying opinions to turn them to the own uses to undermine us, but guerrillas would be led assume responsibilities they could not successfully discharge and that should properly be carried out by orthodox force. In the meantime, the important guerrilla function of co-ordinating activities with the regular forces would be neglected.

Furthermore, if the theory that guerrilla warfare is our only strategy were actually applied, the regular forces would be weakened, we would be divided in purpose, and guerrilla hostilities would decline. If we say, ' Let us transform the regular forces into guerrillas', and do not place our first reliance on a victory to be gained by the regular armies over the enemy, we may certainly expect to see as a result the failure of the anti-Japanese war of resistance. The concept that guerrilla warfare is an end in itself and that guerrilla activities can be divorced from those of the regular forces is incorrect. If we assume that guerrilla warfare does not progress from beginning to end beyond its elementary forms, we have failed to recognize the fact that guerrilla hostilities can, under specific conditions, develop and assume orthodox characteristics. An opinion that admits the existence of guerrilla war, but isolates it, is one that does not properly estimate the potentialities of such war.

Equally dangerous is the concept that condemns guerrilla war on the ground that war has no other aspects than the purely orthodox. This opinion is often expressed by those who have seen the corrupt phenomena of some guerrilla regimes, observed their lack of discipline, and have seen them used as a screen behind which certain persons have indulged in bribery and other corrupt practices. These people will not admit the fundamental necessity for guerrilla bands that spring from the armed people. They say, 'Only the regular forces are capable of conducting guerrilla operations.' This theory is a mistaken one and would lead to the abolition of the people's guerrilla war.

A proper conception of the relationship that exists between guerrilla effort and that of the regular forces is essential. We believe it can be stated this way: 'Guerrilla operations during the anti-Japanese war may for certain time and temporarily become its paramount feature, particularly insofar as the enemy's rear is concerned. However, if we view the war as a whole, there can be no doubt that our regular forces are of primary importance, because it is they who are alone capable of producing the decision. Guerrilla warfare assists them in producing this favorable decision. Orthodox forces may under certain conditions operate as guerrillas, and the latter may, under certain conditions, develop to the status of the former. However, both guerrilla forces and regular forces have their own respective development and their proper combinations.'

To clarify the relationship between the mobile aspect of orthodox war and guerrilla war, we may say that general agreement exists that the principal element of our strategy must be mobility. With the war of movement, we may at times combine the war of position. Both of these are assisted by general guerrilla hostilities. It is true that on the battlefield mobile war often becomes positional; it is true that this situation may be reversed; it is equally true that each form may combine with the other. The possibility of such combination will become more evident after the prevailing standards of equipment have been raised. For example, in a general strategic counter-attack to recapture key cities and lines of communication, it would be normal to use both mobile and positional methods. However, the point must again be made that our fundamental strategic form must be the war of movement. If we deny this, we cannot arrive at the victorious solution of the war. In sum, while we must promote guerrilla warfare as a necessary strategic auxiliary to orthodox operations, we must neither assign it the primary position in our war strategy nor substitute it for mobile and positional warfare as conducted by orthodox forces.

CHAPTER 3

Guerrilla Warfare in History

Guerrilla warfare is neither a product of China nor peculiar to the present day. From the earliest historical days, it has been a feature of wars fought by every class of men against invaders and oppressors. Under suitable conditions, it has great possibilities. The many guerrilla wars in history have their points of difference, their peculiar characteristics, their varying processes and conclusions, and we must respect and profit by the experience of those whose blood was shed in them. What a pity it is that the priceless experience gained during the several hundred wars waged by the peasants of China cannot be marshaled today to guide us. Our only experience in guerrilla hostilities has been that gained from the several conflicts that have been carried on against us by foreign imperialists. But that experience should help the fighting Chinese recognize the necessity for guerrilla warfare and should confirm them in confidence of ultimate victory.

In September 1812, Napoleon, in the course of swallowing all of Europe, invaded Russia at the head of a great army totaling several hundred thousand infantry, cavalry, and artillery. At that time, Russia was weak and her ill-prepared army was not concentrated. The most important phase of her strategy was the use made of Cossack cavalry and detachments of peasants to carry on guerrilla operations. After giving up Moscow, the Russians formed nine guerrilla divisions of about five hundred men each. These, and vast groups of organized peasants, carried on partisan warfare and continually harassed the French Army. When the French Army was withdrawing, cold and starving, Russian guerrillas blocked the way and, in combination with regular troops, carried out counterattacks on the French rear, pursuing and defeating them. The army of the heroic Napoleon was almost entirely annihilated, and the guerrillas captured many officers, men, cannon, and rifles. Though the victory was the result of various factors and depended largely on the activities of the regular army the function of the partisan groups was extremely important. The corrupt and poorly organized country that was Russia defeated and destroyed an army led by the most famous soldier of Europe and won the war in spite of the fact that her ability to organize guerrilla regimes was not fully developed. At times, guerrilla groups were hindered in their operations and the supply of equipment and arms was insufficient. If we use the Russian saying, it was a case of a battle between "the fist and the axe."

From 1918 to 1920, the Russian Soviets, because of the opposition and intervention of foreign imperialists and the internal disturbances of White Russian groups, were forced to organize themselves in occupied territories and fight a real war. In Siberia and Alashan, in the rear of the army of the traitor Denikin and in the rear of the Poles, there were many Red Russian guerrillas. These not only disrupted and destroyed the communications in the enemy's rear but also frequently prevented his advance. On one occasion, the guerrillas completely destroyed a retreating White Army that had previously been defeated by regular Red forces. Kolchak, Denikin, the Japanese, and the Poles, owing to the necessity of staving off the attacks of guerrillas, were forced to withdraw regular troops from the front. 'Thus not only was the enemy's manpower impoverished but he found himself unable to cope with the ever-moving guerrilla'.

The development of guerrillas at that time had only reached the stage where there were detached groups of several thousands in strength, old, middle-aged, and young. The old men organized themselves into propaganda groups known as 'silver-haired units'; there was a suitable guerrilla activity for the middle-aged; the young men formed combat units, and there were even groups for the children. Among the leaders were determined Communists who carried on general political work among the people. These, although they opposed the doctrine of extreme guerrilla warfare, were quick to oppose those who condemned it. Experience tells us that 'Orthodox armies are the fundamental and principal power, guerrilla units are secondary to them and assist in the accomplishment of the mission assigned the regular forces *[Gusev, Lessons of Civil War.]*. Many of the guerrilla regimes in Russia gradually developed until in battle they were able to discharge functions of organized regulars. The army of the famous General Galen was entirely derived from guerrillas.

During seven months in 1935 and 1936, the Abyssinians lost their war against Italy. The cause of defeat — aside from the most important political reasons that there were dissentient political groups, no strong government party, and unstable policy—was the failure to adopt a positive policy of mobile warfare. There was never a combination of the war of movement with large-scale guerrilla operations. Ultimately, the Abyssinians adopted a purely passive defense, with the result that they were unable to defeat the Italians. In addition to this, the fact that Abyssinia is a relatively small and sparsely populated country was contributory. Even in spite of the fact that the Abyssinian Army and its equipment were not modern, she was able to withstand a mechanized Italian force of 400,000 for seven months. During that period, there were several occasions when a war of movement was combined with large-scale guerrilla operations to strike the Italians heavy blows. Moreover, several cities were retaken and casualties totaling 140,000 were inflicted. Had this policy been steadfastly continued, it would have been difficult to have named the ultimate winner. At the present time, guerrilla activities continue in Abyssinia, and if the internal political questions can be solved, an extension of such activities is probable.

In 1841 and 1842, when brave people from San Yuan Li fought the English; again from 1850 to 1864, during the Taiping War, and for a third time in 1899 in the Boxer Uprising, guerrilla tactics were employed to a remarkable degree. Particularly was this so during the Taiping War, when guerrilla operations were most extensive and the Ch'ing troops were often completely exhausted and forced to flee for their lives.

In these wars, there were no guiding principles of guerrilla action. Perhaps these guerrilla hostilities were not carried out in conjunction with regular operations, or perhaps there was a lack of co-ordination. But the fact that victory was not gained was not because of any lack in guerrilla activity but rather because of the interference of politics in military affairs. Experience shows that if precedence is not given to the question of conquering the enemy in both political and military affairs, and if regular hostilities are not conducted with tenacity, guerrilla operations alone cannot produce final victory.

From 1927 to 1936, the Chinese Red Army fought almost continually and employed guerrilla tactics contently. At the very beginning, a positive policy was adopted. Many bases were established, and from guerrilla bands, the Reds were able to develop into regular armies. As these armies fought, new guerrilla regimes were developed over a wide area. These regimes co-ordinated their efforts with those of the regular forces This policy accounted for the many victories gained by the guerrilla troops relatively few in number, who were armed with weapons inferior to those of their opponents. The leaders of that period properly combined guerrilla operations with a war of movement both strategically and tactically. They depended primarily upon alertness. They stressed the correct basis for both political affairs and military operations. They developed their guerrilla bands into trained units. They then determined upon a ten year period of resistance during which time they overcame innumerable difficulties and have only lately reached their goal of direct participation in the anti-Japanese war. There is no doubt that the internal unification of China is now a permanent and definite fact, and that the experience gained during our internal struggles has proved to be both necessary and advantageous to us in the struggle against Japanese imperialism. There are many valuable lessons we can learn from the experience of those years. Principle among them is the fact that guerrilla success largely depend upon powerful political leaders who work unceasingly to bring about internal unification. Such leaders must work with the people; they must have a correct conception of the policy to be adopted as regards both the people and the enemy.

After 18 September 1931, strong anti-Japanese guerrilla campaigns were opened in each of the three north-east provinces. Guerrilla activity persists there in spite of the cruelties and deceits practiced by the Japanese at the expense of the people, and in spite of the fact that her armies have occupied the land and oppressed the people for the last seven years. The struggle can be divided into two periods. During the first, which extended from 18 September 1931 to January 1933, anti-Japanese guerrilla activity exploded constantly in all three provinces. Ma Chan Shan and Su Ping Wei established an anti-Japanese regime in Heilungkiang. In Chi Lin. the National Salvation Army and the Self-Defense Army were led by Wang Te Lin and Li Tu respectively. In Feng T'ien, Chu Lu and others commanded guerrilla units. The influence of these forces was great. They harassed the Japanese unceasingly, but because there was an indefinite political goal, improper leadership, failure to co ordinate military command and operations and to work with the people, and, finally, failure to delegate proper political functions to the army, the whole organization was feeble, and its strength was not unified. As a direct result of these conditions, the campaigns failed and the troops were finally defeated by our enemy.

During the second period, which has extended from January 1933 to the present time, the situation has greatly improved, This has come about because great numbers of people who have been oppressed by the enemy have decided to resist him, because of the participation of the Chinese Communists in the anti-Japanese warm and because of the fine work of the volunteer units. The guerrillas have finally educated the people to the meaning of guerrilla warfare, and in the north-east, it has again become an important and powerful influence. Already seven or eight guerrilla regiments and a number of independent platoons have been formed, and their activities make it necessary for the Japanese to send troops after them month after month. These units hamper the Japanese and undermine their control in the north-east, while, at the same time they inspire a Nationalist revolution in Korea. Such activities are not merely of transient and local importance but directly contribute to our ultimate victory.

However, there are still some weak points. For instance: National defense policy has not been sufficiently developed; participation of the people is not general; internal political organization is still in its primary stages, and the force used to attack the Japanese and the puppet governments is not yet sufficient. But if present policy is continued tenaciously, all these weaknesses will be overcome. Experience proves that guerrilla war will develop to even greater proportions and that, in spite of the cruelty o the Japanese and the many methods they have device to cheat the people, they cannot extinguish guerrilla activities extinguish guerrilla activities in the three north-eastern provinces.

The guerrilla experiences of China and of other countries that have been outlined; prove that in a war of revolutionary nature such hostilities are possible, natural and necessary. They prove that if the present anti-Japanese war for the emancipation of the masses of the Chinese people is to gain ultimate victory, such hostilities must expand tremendously.

Historical experience is written in iron and blood. We must point out that the guerrilla campaigns being waged in China today are a page in history that has no precedent. Their influence will not be confined solely to China in her present anti-Japanese war but will be world-wide.

CHAPTER 4

Can Victory Be Attained By Guerrilla Operations?

Guerrilla hostilities are but one phase of the war of resistance against Japan and the answer to the question of whether or not they can produce ultimate victory can be given only after investigation and comparison of all elements of our own strength with those of the enemy. The particulars of such a comparison are several. First, the strong Japanese bandit nation is an absolute monarchy. During the course of her invasion of China, she had made comparative progress in the techniques of industrial production and in the development of excellence and skill in her army, navy, and air force. But in spite of this industrial progress, she remains an absolute monarchy of inferior physical endowments. Her manpower, her raw materials, and her financial resources are all inadequate and insufficient to maintain her in protracted warfare or to meet the situation presented by a war prosecuted over a vast area. Added to this is the anti-war feeling now manifested by the Japanese people, a feeling that is shared by the junior officers and, more extensively, by the soldiers of the invading army. Furthermore, China is not Japan's only enemy. Japan is unable to employ her entire strength in the attack on China; she cannot, at most, spare more than a million men for this purpose, as she must hold any in excess of that number for use against other possible opponents. Because of these important primary considerations, the invading Japanese bandits can hope neither to be victorious in a protracted struggle nor to conquer a vast area. Their strategy must be one of lightning war and speedy decision. If we can hold out for three or more years, it will be most difficult for Japan to bear up under the strain.

In the war, the Japanese brigands must depend upon lines of communication linking the principal cities as routes for the transport of war materials. The most important considerations for her are that her rear be stable and peaceful and that her lines of communication be intact. It is not to her an advantage to wage war over a vast area with disrupted lines of communication. She cannot disperse her strength and fight in a number of places, and her greatest fears are these eruptions in her rear and disruption of her lines of communication. If she can maintain communications, she will be able at will to concentrate powerful forces speedily at strategic points to engage our organized units in decisive battle. Another important Japanese objective is to profit from the industries, finances, and manpower in captured areas and with them to augment her own insufficient strength. Certainly, it is not to her advantage to forgo these benefits, not to be forced to dissipate her energies in a type of warfare in which the gains will not compensate for the losses. It is for these reasons that guerrilla warfare conducted in each bit of conquered territory over a wide area will be a heavy blow struck at the Japanese bandits. Experience in the five northern provinces as well as in Kiangsu, Chekiang and Anhwei has absolutely established the truth of this assertion.

China is a country half colonial and half feudal; it is a country that is politically, militarily, and economically backward. This is an inescapable conclusion. It is a vast country with great resources and tremendous population, a country in which the terrain is complicated and the facilities for communication are poor. All theses factors favor a protracted war; they all favor the application of mobile warfare and guerilla operations. The establishment of innumerable anti-Japanese bases behind the enemy's lines will force him to fight unceasingly in many places at once, both to his front and his rear. He thus endlessly expends his resources.

Mao Zedong

We must unite the strength of the army with that of the people, we must strike the weak spots in the enemy's flanks, in his front, in his rear. We must make war everywhere and cause dispersal of his forces and dissipation of his strength. Thus the time will come when a gradual change will become evident in the relative position of ourselves and our enemy, and when that day comes, it will be the beginning of our ultimate victory over the Japanese.

Although China's population is great, it is unorganized. This is a weakness which must be then into account.

The Japanese bandits have merely to conquer territory; but continue with a murderous policy of the extinction of the Chinese race. We must unite the nation without regard to parties and follow our policy of resistance to the end. China today is not the China of old. It is not like Abyssinia. China today is at the point of her greatest historical progress. The standards of literacy among the masses have been raised; the *rapprochement* of Communists and Nationalists has laid the foundation for an anti-Japanese war front that is constantly being strengthened and expanded; government, army and people are all working with great energy; the raw material resources and the economic strength of the nation are waiting to be used; the unorganized people are becoming an organized nation.

These energies must be directed toward the goal of protracted war so that should the Japanese occupy much of our territory or even most of it, we shall still gain final victory. Not only must those behind our lines organize for resistance but also those who live in Japanese-occupied territory in every part of the country. The traitors who accept the Japanese as fathers are few in number, and those who have taken oath that they would prefer death to abject slavery are many. If we resist with this spirit, what enemy can we not conquer and who can say that ultimate victory will not be ours?

The Japanese are waging a barbaric war along uncivilized lines. For that reason, Japanese of all classes oppose the policies of their government, as do vast international groups. On the other hand, because China's cause is righteous, our countrymen of all classes and parties are united to oppose the invader; we have sympathy in many foreign countries including even Japan itself. This is perhaps the most important reason why Japan will lose and China will win.

The progress of the war for the emancipation of the Chinese people will be in accord with these facts. The guerrilla war of resistance will be in accord with these facts, and that guerrilla operations correlated with those of our regular forces will produce victory is the conviction of the many patriots who devote their entire strength to guerrilla hostilities.

CHAPTER 5

Organization for Guerilla Warfare

Four points must be considered. These are:

How are guerrilla bands formed?
How are guerrilla bands organized?
What are the methods of arming guerrilla bands?
What elements constitute a guerrilla band?

These are all questions pertaining to the organization armed guerrilla units; they are questions which those who had no experience in guerilla hostilities do not understand and on which they can arrive at no sound decisions; indeed, they would not know in what manner to begin.

How Guerrilla Units Are Originally Formed

The unit may originate in any one of the following ways:

a) From the masses of the people.
b) From regular army units temporarily detailed for the purpose.
c) From regular army units permanently detailed.
d) From the combination of a regular army unit and a unit recruited from the people.
e) From the local militia.
f) From deserters from the ranks of the enemy.
g) From former bandits and bandit groups.

In the present hostilities, no doubt, all these sources will be employed.

In the first case above, the guerrilla unit is formed from the people. This is the fundamental type. Upon the arrival of the enemy army to oppress and slaughter the people, their leaders call upon them to resist. They assemble the most valorous elements, arm them with old rifles or whatever firearms they can, and thus a guerrilla unit begins. Orders have already been issued throughout the nation, that call upon the people to form guerrilla units both for local defense and for other combat. If the local governments approve and aid such movements, they cannot fail to prosper. In some places, where the local government is not determined or where its officers have all fled, the leaders among the masses (relying on the sympathy of the people and their sincere desire to resist Japan and succor the country) call upon the people to resist, and they respond. Thus, many guerrilla units are organized. In circumstances of this kind, the duties of leadership usually fall upon the shoulders of young students, teachers, professors, other educators, local soldiery, professional men, artisans, and those without a fixed profession, who are willing to exert themselves to the last drop of their blood. Recently, in Shansi, Hopeh, Chahar, Suiyuan, Shantung, Chekiang, Anhwei, Kiangsu, and other provinces, extensive guerrilla hostilities have broken out. All these are organized and led by patriots. The amount of such activity is the best proof of the foregoing statement. The more such bands there are, the better will the situation be. Each district, each county, should be able to organize a great number of guerrilla squads, which, when assembled, form a guerrilla company.

There are those who say: 'I am a farmer', or, 'I am a student'; 'I can discuss literature but not military arts.' This is incorrect. There is no profound difference between the farmer and the soldier. You must have courage. You simply leave your farms and become soldiers. That you are farmers is of no difference, and if you have education, that is so much the better. When you take your arms in hand, you become soldiers; when you are organized, you become military units.

Guerrilla hostilities are the university of war, and after you have fought several times valiantly and aggressively, you may become a leader of troops and there will be many well-known regular soldiers who will not be your peers. Without question, the fountainhead of guerrilla warfare is in the masses of the people, who organize guerrilla units directly from themselves.

The second type of guerrilla unit is that which is organized from small units of the regular forces temporarily detached for the purpose. For example, since hostilities commenced, many groups have been temporarily detached from armies, divisions, and brigades and have been assigned guerrilla duties. A regiment of the regular army may, if circumstances warrant, be dispersed into groups for the purpose of carrying on guerrilla operations. As an example of this, there is the Eighth Route Army, in North China. Excluding the periods when it carries on mobile operations as an army, it is divided into its elements and these carry on guerrilla hostilities. This type of guerrilla unit is essential for two reasons. First, in mobile-warfare situations, the co-ordination of guerrilla activities with regular operations is necessary. Second, until guerrilla hostilities can be developed on a grand scale, there is no one to carry out guerrilla missions but regulars. Historical experience shows us that regular army units are not able to undergo the hardships of guerrilla campaigning over long periods. The leaders of regular units engaged in guerrilla operations must be extremely adaptable. They must study the methods of guerrilla war. They must understand that initiative, discipline, and the employment of stratagems are all of the utmost importance. As the guerrilla status of regular units is but temporary, their leaders must lend all possible support to the organization of guerrilla units from among the people. These units must be so disciplined that they hold together after the departure of the regulars.

The third type of unit consists of a detachment of regulars who are permanently assigned guerrilla duties. This type of small detachment does not have to be prepared to rejoin the regular forces. Its post is somewhere in the rear of the enemy, and there it becomes the backbone of guerrilla organization. As an example of this type of organization we may take the Wu Tat Shan district in the heart of the Hopeh-Chahar-Shansi area. Along the borders of these provinces, units from the Eighth Route Army have established a framework or guerrilla operations. Around these small cores, many detachments have been organized and the area of guerrilla activity greatly expanded. In areas in which there is a possibility of cutting the enemy's lines of supply, this system should be used. Severing enemy, supply routes destroys his lifeline; this is one feature that cannot be neglected. If, at the time the regular forces withdraw from a certain area, some units left behind, these should conduct guerrilla operations in the enemy's rear. As an example of this, we have the guerrilla bands now continuing their independent operations in the Shanghai-Woosung area in spite of the withdrawal of regular forces.

The fourth type of organization is the result of a merger between small regular detachments and local guerrilla units. The regular forces may dispatch a squad, a platoon, or a company, which is placed at the disposal of the local guerrilla commander. If a small group experienced in military and political affairs is sent, it becomes the core of the local guerrilla unit. These several methods are all excellent, and if properly applied, the intensity of guerilla warfare can be extended. In the Wu Tat Shan area, each of these methods has been used.

The fifth type mentioned above is from the local militia, from police and home guards. In every North China province, there are now many of these groups, and they should be formed in every locality. The government has issued mandate to the effect that the people are not to depart from war areas. The officer in command of the county, the commander of the peace-preservation unit, the chief of police are all required to obey this mandate. They cannot retreat with their forces but must remain at their stations and resist.

The sixth type of unit is that organized from troops that come over from the enemy—the Chinese 'traitor' troops employed by the Japanese. It is always possible to produce disaffection in their ranks, and we must increase our propaganda efforts and foment mutinies among such troops. Immediately after mutinying, they must be received into our ranks and organized. The concord of the leaders and the assent of the men must be gained, and the units rebuilt politically and reorganized militarily. Once this has been accomplished, they become successful guerrilla units. In regard to this type of unit, it may be said that political work among them is of utmost importance.

The seventh type of guerrilla organization is that formed from bands of bandits and brigands. This, although difficult, must be carried out with utmost vigor lest the enemy use such bands to his own advantages. Many bandit groups pose as anti-Japanese guerrillas, and it is only necessary to correct their political beliefs to convert them.

In spite of inescapable differences in the fundamental types of guerrilla bands, it is possible to unite them to form a vast sea of guerrillas. The ancients said, 'Tai Shan is a great mountain because it does not scorn the merest handful of dirt; the rivers and seas are deep because they absorb the waters of small streams.' Attention paid to the enlistment and organization of guerrillas of every type and from every source will increase the potentialities of guerrilla action in the anti-Japanese war. This is something that patriots will not neglect.

THE METHOD OF ORGANIZING GUERRILLA REGIMES

Many of those who decide to participate in guerrilla activities do not know the methods of organization. For such people, as well as for students who have no knowledge of military affairs, the matter of organization is a problem that requires solution. Even among those who have military knowledge, there are some who know nothing of guerrilla regimes use they are lacking in that particular type of experience. The subject of the organization of such regimes is not confined to the organization of specific units but includes all guerrilla activities within the area where the regime functions.

As an example of such organization, we may take a geographical area in the enemy's rear. This area may comprise many counties. It must be sub-divided and individual companies or battalions formed to accord with the sub-divisions. To this 'military area', a military commander and political commissioners are appointed. Under these, the necessary officers both military and political, are appointed. In the military headquarters, there will be the staff, the aides, the supply officers, and the medical personnel. These are controlled by the chief of staff, who acts in accordance with orders from the commander. In the political headquarters, there are bureaus of propaganda organization, people's mass movements, and miscellaneous affairs. Control of these is vested in the political chairman.

The military areas are sub-divided into smaller districts in accordance with local geography, the enemy situation locally, and the state of guerrilla development. Each of these smaller divisions within the area is a district, each of which may consist of from two to six counties. To each district, a military commander and several political commissioners are appointed. Under their direction, military and political headquarters are organized. Tasks are assigned in accordance with the number of guerrilla troops available. Although the names of the officers in the 'district' correspond to those in the larger 'area', the number of the functionaries assigned in the former case should be reduced to the least possible. In order to unify control, to handle guerrilla troops that come from different sources, and to harmonize military operations and local political affairs, a committee of from seven to nine members should be organized in each area and district. This committee, the members of which are selected by the troops and the local political officers, should function as a forum for the discussion of both military and political matters.

All the people in an area should arm themselves and be organized into two groups. One of these groups is a combat group, the other a self-defense unit with but limited military quality. Regular combatant guerrillas are organized into one of three general types of units. The first of these is the small unit, the platoon or company. In each county, three to six units may be organized. The second type is the battalion of from two to four companies. One such unit should be organized in each county. While the unit fundamentally belongs to the county in it was organized, it may operate in other counties. While in areas other than its own, it must operate in conjunction with local units in order to take advantage of their manpower, their knowledge of local terrain and local customs, and their information of the enemy.

The third type is the guerrilla regiment, which consists of from two to four of the above-mentioned battalion units. If sufficient manpower is available, a guerrilla a brigade of from two to four regiments may be formed.

Each of the units has its own peculiarities of organization. A squad, the smallest unit, has a strength of from nine to eleven men, including the leader and the assistant leader. Its arms may be from two to five Western-style rifles, with the remaining men armed with rifles of local manufacture, fowling-pieces, etc., spears, or big swords. Two to four such squads form a platoon. This too has a leader and an assistant leader, and when acting independently, it is assigned a political officer to carry on political propaganda work. The platoon may have about ten rifles, with the remainder of its four of such units from a company, which, like the platoon, has a leader, an assistant leader, and a political officer. All these units are under the direct supervision of the military commanders of the areas in which they operate.

The battalion unit must be more thoroughly organized and better equipped than the smaller units. Its discipline and its personnel should be superior. If a battalion is formed from company units, it should not deprive subordinate units entirely of their manpower and their arms. If in a small area, there is a peace-preservation corps, a branch of the militia, or police, regular guerrilla units should not be dispersed over it.

The guerrilla unit next in size to the battalion is the regiment. This must be under more severe discipline than the battalion. In an independent guerrilla regiment, there may be ten men per squad, three squad per platoon, three platoons per company, three companies per battalion, and three battalions to the regiment. Two of such regiments form a brigade. Each of these units has a commander, a vice-commander, and a political officer.

In North China, guerrilla cavalry units should be established. These may be regiments of from two to four companies, or battalions.

All these units from the lowest to the highest are combatant guerrilla units and receive their supplies from the central government. Details of their organization are shown in the tables.

All the people of both sexes from the ages of sixteen to forty-five must be organized into anti-Japanese self-defense units, the basis of which is voluntary service. As a first step, they must procure arms, then they must be given both military and political training. Their responsibilities are: local sentry duties, securing information of the enemy, arresting traitors, and preventing the dissemination of enemy propaganda. When the enemy launches a guerrilla-suppression drive, these units, armed with what weapons there are, are assigned to certain areas to deceive, hinder, and harass him. Thus, the defense units assist the combatant guerrillas. They have other functions. They furnish stretcher-bearers to transport the wounded, carriers to take food to the troops, and comfort missions to provide the troops with tea and rice. If a locality can organize such a self-defense unit as we have described, the traitors cannot hide nor can bandits and robbers disturb the peace of the people. Thus the people will continue to assist the guerrilla and supply manpower to our regular armies. 'The organization of self-defense units is a transitional step in the development of universal conscription. Such units are reservoirs of manpower for the orthodox forces.'

There have been such organizations for some time in Shansi, Shensi, Honan, and Suiyuan. The youth organizations in different provinces were formed for the purpose of educating the young. They have been of some help. However, they were not voluntary, and confidence of the people was thus not gained. These organizations were not widespread, and their effect was almost negligible. This system was, therefore, supplanted by the new-type organizations,. Which are organized on the principles of voluntary co-operation and non-separation of the members from their native localities. When the members of these organizations are in their native towns, they support themselves. Only in case of military necessity are they ordered to remote places, and when this is done, the government must support them. Each member of these groups must have a weapon even if the weapon is only a knife, a pistol, a lance, or a spear.

In all places where the enemy operates, these self-defense units should organize within themselves a small guerrilla group of perhaps from three to ten men armed with pistols or revolvers. This group is not required to leave its native locality.

The organization of these self-defense units is mentioned in this book because such units are useful for the purposes of inculcating the people with military and political knowledge, keeping order in the rear, and replenishing the ranks of the regulars. These groups should be organized not only in the active war zones but in every province in China. 'The people must be inspired to co-operate voluntarily. We must not force them, for if we do, it will be ineffectual.' This is extremely important.

In order to control anti-Japanese military organization as a whole, it is necessary to establish a system of military areas and districts along the lines we have indicated.

EQUIPMENT OF GUERRILLAS

In regard to the problem of guerrilla equipment, it must be understood that guerrillas are lightly-armed attack groups, which require simple equipment. The standard of equipment is based upon the nature of duties assigned; the equipment of low-class guerrilla units is not as good as that of higher-class units. For example, those who are assigned the task of destroying rail communications are better equipped than those who do not have that task. The equipment of guerrillas cannot be based on what the guerrillas want, to even what they need, but must be based on what is available for their use. Equipment cannot be furnished immediately but must be acquired gradually. These are points to be kept in mind.

The question of equipment includes the collection, supply, distribution, and replacement of weapons, ammunition, blankets, communication materials, transport, and facilities for propaganda work. The supply of weapons and ammunition is most difficult, particularly at the time the unit is established, but this problem can always be solved eventually. Guerrilla bands that originate in the people are furnished with revolvers, pistols, rifles, spears, big swords, and land mines and mortars of local manufacture. Other elementary weapons are added and as many new-type rifles as are available are distributed. After a period of resistance, it is possible to increase the supply of equipment by capturing it from the enemy. In this respect, the transport companies are the easiest to equip, for in any successful attack, we will capture the enemy's transport.

An armory should be established in each guerrilla district for the manufacture and repair of rifles and for the production of cartridge, hand grenades and bayonets. Guerrillas must not depend too much on an armory. The enemy is the principal source of their supply.

For destruction of railway tracks, bridges, and stations in enemy-controlled territory, it is necessary to gather together demolition materials. Troops must be trained in the preparation and use of demolitions, and a demolition unit must be organized in each regiment.

As for minimum clothing requirements, these are that each man shall have at least two summer-weight uniforms, one suit of winter clothing, two hats, a pair of wrap puttees, and blanket. Each man must have a pack or a bag for food. In the north, each man must have an overcoat. In acquiring this clothing, we cannot depend on captures made by the enemy, for it is forbidden for captors to take clothing from their prisoners. In order to maintain high morale in guerrilla forces, all the clothing and equipment mentioned should be furnished by the representatives of the government in each guerrilla district. These men may confiscate clothing from traitors or ask contributions from those best able to afford them. In subordinate groups, uniforms are unnecessary.

Telephone and radio equipment is not necessary in lower groups, but all units from regiment up are equipped with both. This material can be obtained by contributions from the regular forces and by capture from the enemy.

In the guerrilla army in general, and at bases in particular, there must be a high standard of medical equipment. Besides the services of the doctors, medicines must be procured. Although guerrillas can depend on the enemy for some portion of their medical supplies, they must, in general, depend upon contributions. If Western medicines are not available, local medicines must be made to suffice.

The problem of transport is more vital in North-China than in the south, for in the south all that are necessary are mules and horses. Small guerrilla units need no animals, but regiments and brigades will find them necessary. Commanders and staffs of units from companies up should be furnished a riding animal each. At times, two officers will have to share a horse. Officers whose duties are of minor nature do not have to be mounted.

Propaganda materials are very important. Every large guerrilla unit should have a printing press and a mimeograph stone. They must also have paper on which to print propaganda leaflets and notices. They must be supplied with large brushes. In guerrilla areas, there should be a printing press or a lead-type press.

For the purpose of printing training instructions, this material is of the greatest importance.

In addition to the equipment listed above, it is necessary to have field-glasses, compasses, and military maps. An accomplished guerrilla group will acquire these things.

Because of the proved importance of guerrilla hostilities in the anti-Japanese war, the headquarters of the Nationalist Government and the commanding officers of the various war zones should do their best to supply the guerrillas with what they actually need and are unable to get for themselves. However, it must be repeated that guerrilla equipment will in the main depend on the efforts of the guerrillas themselves. If they depend on higher officers too much, the psychological effect will be to weaken the guerrilla spirit of resistance.

ELEMENTS OF THE GUERRILLA ARMY

The term 'element' as used in the title to this section refers to the personnel, both officers and men, of the guerrilla army. Since each guerrilla group fights in a protracted war, its officers must be brave and positive men whose entire loyalty is dedicated to the cause of emancipation of the people. An officer should have the following qualities: great powers of endurance so that in spite of any hardship he sets an example to his men and be a model for them; he must be able to mix easily with the people; his spirit and that of the men must be one in strengthening the policy of resistance to the Japanese. If he wishes to gain victories, he must study tactics. A guerrilla group with officers of this caliber would be unbeatable. I do not mean that every guerrilla group can have, at its inception, officers of such qualities. The officers must be men naturally endowed with good qualities which can be developed during the course of campaigning. The most important natural quality is that of complete loyalty to the idea of people's emancipation. If this is present, the others will develop; if it is not present, nothing can be done. When officers are first selected from a group, it is this quality that should receive particular attention.

The officers in a group should be inhabitants of the locality in which the group is organized, as this will facilitate relations between them and the local civilians. In addition, officers so chosen would be familiar with conditions. If in any locality there are not enough men of sufficiently high qualifications to become officers, an effort must be made to train and educate the people so these qualities may be developed and the potential officer material increased. There can be no disagreements between officers native to one place and those from other localities.

A guerrilla group ought to operate on the principle that only volunteers are acceptable for service. It is a mistake to impress people into service. As long as a person is willing to fight, his social condition or position is no consideration, but only men who are courageous and determined can bear the hardships of guerrilla campaigning in a protracted war.

A soldier who habitually breaks regulations must be dismissed from the army. Vagabonds and vicious people must not be accepted for service. The opium habit must be forbidden, and a soldier who cannot break himself of the habit should be dismissed. Victory in guerrilla war is conditioned upon keeping the membership pure and clean.

It is a fact that during the war the enemy may take advantage of certain people who are lacking in conscience and patriotism and induce them to join the guerrillas for the purpose of betraying them. Officers must, therefore, continually educate the soldiers and inculcate patriotism in them. This will prevent the success of traitors. The traitors who are in the ranks must be discovered and expelled, and punishment and expulsion meted out to those who have been influenced by them. In all such cases, the officers should summon the soldiers and relate the facts to them, thus arousing their hatred and detestation for traitors. This procedure will serve as well as a warning to the other soldiers. If an officer is discovered to be a traitor, some prudence must be used in the punishment adjudged. However, the work of eliminating traitors in the army begins with their elimination from among the people.

Chinese soldiers who have served under puppet governments and bandits who have been converted should be welcomed as individuals or as groups. They should be well-treated and repatriated. But care should be used during their reorientation to distinguish those whose idea is to fight the Japanese from those who may be present for other reasons.

CHAPTER 6

The Political Problems of Guerrilla Warfare

I mentioned the fact that guerrilla troops should have a precise conception of the political goal of the struggle and the political organization to be used in attaining that goal. This means that both organization and discipline of guerrilla troops must be at a high level so that they can carry out the political activities that are the life of both the guerilla armies and of revolutionary warfare.

First of all, political activities depend upon the indoctrination of both military and political leaders with the idea of anti-Japanism. Through them, the idea is transmitted to the troops. One must not feel that he is anti-Japanese merely because he is a member of a guerrilla unit. The anti-Japanese idea must be an ever-present conviction, and if it is forgotten, we may succumb to the temptations of the enemy or be overcome with discouragement. In a war of long duration, those whose conviction that the people must be emancipated is not deep rooted are likely to become shaken in their faith or actually revolt. Without the general education that enables everyone to understand our goal of driving out Japanese imperialism and establishing a free and happy China, the soldiers fight without conviction and lose their determination.

The political goal must be clearly and precisely indicated to inhabitants of guerrilla zones and their national consciousness awakened. Hence, a concrete explanation of the political systems used is important not only to guerrilla troops but to all those who are concerned with the realization of our political goal. The Kuomintang has issued a pamphlet entitled

System of National Organization for War, which should be widely distributed throughout guerrilla zones. If we lack national organization, we will lack the essential unity that should exist between the soldiers and the people.

A study and comprehension of the political objectives of this war and of the anti-Japanese front is particularly important for officers of guerrilla troops. There are some militarists who say: 'We are not interested in politics but only in the profession of arms.' It is vital that these simple-minded militarists be made to realize the relationship that exists between politics and military affairs. Military action is a method used to attain a political goal. While military affairs and political affairs are not identical, it is impossible to isolate one from the other.

It is to be hoped that the world is in the last era of strife. The vast majority of human beings have already prepared or are preparing to fight a war that will bring justice to the oppressed peopled of the world. No matter how long this war may last, there is no doubt that it will be followed by an unprecedented epoch of peace The war that we are fighting today for the freedom of all human beings, and the independent, happy, and liberal China that we are fighting to establish will be a part of that new world order. A conception like this is difficult for the simple-minded militarist to grasp and it must therefore be carefully explained to him.

There are three additional matters that must be considered under the broad question of political activities. These are political activities, first, as applied to the troops; second, as applied to the people; and, third, as applied to the enemy. The fundamental problems are: first, spiritual unification of officers and men within the army; second spiritual unification of the army and the people; of the army and the people; and, last, destruction of the unity of the enemy. The concrete methods for achieving these unities are discussed in detail in pamphlet Number 4 of this series, entitled *Political Activities in Anti-Japanese Guerrilla Warfare.*

A revolutionary army must have discipline that is established on a limited democratic basis. In all armies, obedience the subordinates to their superiors must be exacted. This is true in the case of guerrilla discipline, but the basis for guerrilla discipline must be the individual conscience. With guerrillas, a discipline of compulsion is ineffective. In any revolutionary army, there is unity of purpose as far as both officers and men are concerned, and, therefore, within such an army, discipline is self-imposed. Although discipline in guerrilla ranks is not as severe as in the ranks of orthodox forces, the necessity for discipline exists. This must be self-imposed, because only when it is, is the soldier able to understand completely, why he fights and why he must obey. This type of discipline becomes a tower of strength within the army, and it is the only type that can truly harmonize the relationship that exists between officers and soldiers.

In any system where discipline is externally imposed, the relationship that exists between officer and man is characterized by indifference of the one to the other. The idea that officers can physically beat or severely tongue-lash their men is a feudal one and is not in accord with the conception of self-imposed discipline. Discipline of the feudal type will destroy internal unity and fighting strength. A discipline self-imposed is the primary characteristic of a democratic system in the army.

A secondary characteristic is found in the degree of liberties accorded officers and soldiers. In a revolutionary army, all individuals enjoy political liberty and the question, for example, of the emancipation of the people must not only be tolerated but discussed, and propaganda must be encouraged. Further, in such an army, the mode of living of the officers and the soldiers must not differ too much, and this is particularly true in the case of guerilla troops. Officers should live under the same conditions as their men, for that is the only way in which they can gain from their men the admiration and confidence so vital in war. It is incorrect to hold to a theory of equality in all things. But there must be equality of existence in accepting the hardships and dangers of war, thus we may attain to the unification of the officer and soldier groups a unity both horizontal within the group itself, and vertical, that is, from lower to higher echelons. It is only when such unity is present that units can be said to be powerful combat factors.

There is also a unity of spirit that should exist between troops and local inhabitants. The Eighth Route Army put into practice a code known as 'Three Rules and the Eight Remarks', which we list here:

Rules:

All actions are subject to command.
Do not steal from the people.
Be neither selfish nor unjust.

Remarks:

Replace the door when you leave the house.
Roll up the bedding on which you have slept.
Be courteous.
Be honest in your transactions.
Return what you borrow.
Replace what you break.

Do not bathe in the presence of women.
Do not without authority search those you arrest.

The Red Army adhered to this code for ten years and the Eighth Route Army and other units have since adopted it.

Many people think it impossible for guerrillas to exist for long in the enemy's rear. Such a belief reveals lack of comprehension of the relationship that should exist between the people and the troops. The former may be likened to water the latter to the fish which inhabit it. How may it be said that these two cannot exist together? It is only undisciplined troops who make the people their enemies and who, like the fish out of its native element cannot live.

We further our mission of destroying the enemy by propagandizing his troops, by treating his captured soldiers with consideration, and by caring for those of his wounded who fall into our hands. If we fail in these respects, we strengthen the solidarity of our enemy.

CHAPTER 7

The Strategy of Guerrilla Resistance against Japan

It has been definitely decided that in the strategy of our war against Japan, guerrilla strategy must be auxiliary to fundamental orthodox methods. If this were a small country, guerrilla activities could be carried out close to the scene of operations of the regular army and directly complementary to them. In such a case, there would be no question of guerrilla strategy as such. Nor would the question arise if our country were as strong as Russia, for example, and able speedily to eject an invader. The question exists because China, a weak country of vast size, has today progressed to the point where it has become possible to adopt the policy of a protracted war characterized by guerrilla operations. Although these may at first glance seem to be abnormal or heterodox, such is not actually the case.

Because Japanese military power is inadequate, much of the territory her armies have overrun is without sufficient garrison troops. Under such circumstances the primary functions of guerrillas are three: first, to conduct a war on exterior lines, that is, in the rear of the enemy; second, to establish bases, and, last, to extend the war areas. Thus, guerrilla participation in the war is not merely a matter of purely local guerrilla tactics but involves strategic considerations.

Such war, with its vast time and space factors, establishes a new military process, the focal point of which is China today. The Japanese are apparently attempting to recall a past that saw the Yuan extinguish the Sung and the Ch'ing conquer the Ming; that witnessed the extension of the British Empire to North America and India; that saw the Latins overrun Central and South America. As far as China today is concerned, such dreams of conquest are fantastic and without reality. Today's China is better equipped than was the China of yesterday, and a new type of guerrilla hostilities is a part of that equipment. If our enemy fails to take these facts into consideration and makes too optimistic an estimate of the situation, he courts disaster.

Though the strategy of guerrillas is inseparable from war strategy as a whole, the actual conduct of these hostilities differs from the conduct of orthodox operations. Each type of warfare has methods peculiar to itself, and methods suitable to regular warfare cannot be applied with success to the special situations that confront guerrillas.

Before we treat the practical aspects of guerrilla war, it might be well to recall the fundamental axiom of combat on which all military action is based. This can be stated: 'Conservation of one's own strength; destruction of enemy strength.' A military policy based on this axiom is consonant with a national policy directed towards the building of a free and prosperous Chinese state and the destruction of Japanese imperialism. It is in furtherance of this policy that government applies in military strength. Is the sacrifice demanded by war in conflict with the idea of self-preservation? Not at all. The sacrifices demanded are necessary both to destroy the enemy and to preserve ourselves; the sacrifice of a part of the people is necessary to preserve the whole. All the considerations of military action are derived from this axiom. Its application is as apparent in all tactical and strategic conceptions as it is in the simple case of the soldier who shoots at his enemy from a covered position.

All guerrilla units start from nothing and grow. What methods should we select to ensure the conservation and development of our own strength and the destruction of that of the enemy? The essential requirements are the six listed below:

1. Retention of the initiative; alertness; carefully planned tactical attacks in a war of strategic defense; tactical speed in a war strategically protracted, tactical operations on exterior lines in a war conducts strategically on interior lines.
2. Conduct of operations to complement those of the regular army.
3. The establishment of bases.
4. A clear understanding of the relationship that exists between the attack and the defense.
5. The development of mobile operations.
6. Correct command.

The enemy, though numerically weak, is strong in the quality of his troops and their equipment; we, on the other hand, are strong numerically but weak as to quality. These considerations have been taken into account in the development of the policy of tactical offence, tactical speed, and tactical operations on exterior lines in a war that, strategically speaking, is defensive in character, protracted in nature, and conducted along interior lines. Our strategy is based on these conceptions. They must be kept in mind in the conduct of all operations.

Although the element of surprise is not absent in orthodox warfare, there are fewer opportunities to apply it than there are during guerrilla hostilities. In the latter, speed is essential. The movements of guerrilla troops must be secret and of supernatural rapidity; the enemy must be taken unaware, and the action entered speedily. There can be no procrastination in the execution of plans; no assumption of a negative or passive defense; no great dispersion of forces in many local engagements. The basic method is the attack in a violent and deceptive form.

While there may be cases where the attack will extend over a period of several days (if that length of time in necessary to annihilate an enemy group), it is more profitable to launch and push an attack with maximum speed. The tactics of defense have no place in the realm of guerrilla warfare. If a delaying action is necessary, such places as defiles, river crossings, and villages offer the most suitable conditions, for it is in such places that the enemy's arrangements may be disrupted and he may be annihilated.

The enemy is much stronger than we are, and it is true that we can hinder, distract, disperse, and destroy him only if we disperse our own forces. Although guerrilla warfare is the warfare of such dispersed units, it is sometimes desirable to concentrate in order to destroy an enemy. Thus, the principle of concentration of force against a relatively weaker enemy is applicable to guerrilla warfare.

We can prolong this struggle and make of it a protracted war only by gaining positive and lightning-like tactical decisions; by employing our manpower in proper concentrations and dispersions; and by operation on exterior lines in order to surround and destroy our enemy. If we cannot surround whole armies, we can at least partially destroy them, if we cannot kill the Japanese, we can capture them. The total effect of many local successes will be to change the relative strengths of the opposing forces. The destruction of Japan's military power, combined with the international sympathy for China's cause and the revolutionary tendencies evident in Japan, will be sufficient to destroy Japanese imperialism.

We will next discuss initiative, alertness, and the matter of careful planning. What is meant by initiative in warfare? In all battles and wars, a struggle to gain and retain the initiative goes on between the opposing sides, for it is the side that holds the initiative that has liberty of action. When an army loses the initiative, it loses its liberty; its role becomes passive; it faces the danger of defeat and destruction.

It is more difficult to obtain the initiative when defending on interior lines than it is while attacking on exterior lines. This is what Japan is doing. There are, however, several weak points as far as Japan is concerned. One of these is lack of sufficient manpower for the task; another is her cruelty to the inhabitants of conquered areas; a third is the underestimation of Chinese strength, which has resulted in the differences between military cliques, which, in turn, have been productive of many mistakes in the direction of her military forces. For instance, she has been gradually compelled to increase her manpower in China while, at the same time, the many arguments over plans of operations and disposition of troops have resulted in the loss of good opportunities for improvement of her strategic position.

This explains the fact that although the Japanese are frequently able to surround large bodies of Chinese troops, they have never yet been able to capture more than a few. The Japanese military machine is thus being weakened by insufficiency of manpower, inadequacy of resources, the barbarism of her troops, and the general stupidity that has characterized the conduct of operations. Her offensive continues unabated, but because of the weaknesses pointed out, her attack must be limited in extent. She can never conquer China. The day will come — indeed already has in some areas — when she will be forced into a passive role. When hostilities commenced, China was passive, but as we enter the second phase of the war we find ourselves pursuing a strategy of mobile warfare, with both guerrillas and regulars operating on exterior lines. Thus, with each passing day, we seize some degree of initiative from the Japanese.

The matter of initiative is especially serious for guerrilla forces; who must face critical situations unknown to regular troops. The superiority of the enemy and the lack of unity and experience within our own ranks may be cited. Guerrillas can, however, gain the initiative if they keep in mind the weak points of the enemy. Because of the enemy's insufficient manpower, guerrillas can operate over vast territories, because he is a foreigner and a barbarian, guerrillas can gain the confidence of millions of their countrymen; because of the stupidity of enemy commanders, guerrillas can make full use of their own cleverness. Both guerrillas and regulars must exploit these enemy weaknesses while, at the same time, our own are remedied. Some of our weaknesses are apparent only and are, in actuality, sources of strength. For example, the very fact that most guerrilla groups are small makes it desirable and advantageous for them to appear and disappear in the enemy's rear. With such activities, the enemy is simply unable to cope. A similar liberty of action can rarely be obtained by regular forces.

When the enemy attacks the guerrillas with more than one column, it is difficult for the latter to retain the initiative. Any error, no matter how slight, in the estimation of the situation is likely to result in forcing the guerrillas into a passive role. They will then find themselves unable to fend off the attacks of the enemy.

It is apparent that we can gain and retain the initiative only by a correct estimation of the situation and a proper arrangement of all military and political factors. A too pessimistic estimate will operate to force us into a passive position, with consequent loss of initiative; an overly optimistic estimate, with its rash ordering of factors, will produce the same result.

No military leader is endowed by heaven with an ability to seize the initiative. It is the intelligent leader who does so after a careful study and estimate of the situation and arrangement of the military and political factors involved. When a guerrilla unit, through either a poor estimate on the part of its leader or pressure from the enemy, is forced into a passive position, its first duty is to extricate itself. No method can be prescribed for this, as the method to be employed will, in every case, depend on the situation. One can, if necessary, run away. But there are times when the situation seems hopeless and, in reality, is not so at all. It is at such times that the good leader recognizes and seizes the moment when he can regain the lost initiative.

Let us revert to alertness. To conduct one's troops with alertness is an essential of guerrilla command. Leaders must realize that to operate alertly is the most important factor in gaining the initiative and vital in its effect of the relative situation that exists between our forces and those of the enemy. Guerrilla commanders adjust their operations to the enemy situation, to the terrain, and to prevailing local conditions. Leaders must be alert to sense changes in these factors and make necessary modifications in troop dispositions to accord with them. The leader must be like a fisherman, who, with his nets, is able both to cast them and to pull them out in awareness of the depth of the water, the strength of the current or the presence of any obstructions that may foul them. As the fisherman controls his nets through the lead ropes, so the guerrilla leader maintains contact with control over his units. As the fisherman must change his position, so must the guerrilla commander. Dispersion, concentration, constant change of position—it is in these ways that guerrillas employ, their strength.

In general, guerrilla units disperse to operate:

1. When the enemy is in over-extended defense, and sufficient force cannot be concentrated against him, guerrillas must disperse, harass him, and demoralize him.
2. When encircled by the enemy, guerrillas disperse to withdraw.
3. When the nature of the ground limits action, guerrillas disperse.
4. When the availability of supplies limits action, they disperse.
5. Guerrillas disperse in order to promote mass movements over a wide area.

Regardless of the circumstances that prevail at the time of dispersal, caution must be exercised in certain matters:

A relatively large group should be retained as a central force. The remainder of the troops should not be divided into groups of absolutely equal size. In this way, the leader is in a position to deal with any circumstances that may arise. Each dispersed unit should have clear and definite responsibilities. Orders should specify a place to which to proceed, the time of proceeding, and the place, time, and method of assembly.

Guerrillas concentrate when the enemy is advancing upon them, and there is opportunity to fall upon him and destroy him. Concentration may be desirable when the enemy is on the defensive and guerrillas wish to destroy isolated detachments in particular localities. By the term 'concentrate', we do not mean the assembly of all manpower but rather of only that necessary for the task. The remaining guerrillas are assigned missions of hindering and delaying the enemy, of destroys isolated groups, or of conducting mass propaganda.

In addition to the dispersion and concentration of forces, the leader must understand what is termed 'alert shifting'. When the enemy feels the danger of guerrillas, he will generally send troops out to attack them. The guerrillas must consider the situation and decide at what time and at what place they wish to fight. If they find that they cannot fight, they must immediately shift. Then the enemy may be destroyed piecemeal. For example; after a guerrilla group has destroyed an enemy detachment at one place, it may be shifted to another area to attack and destroy a second detachment. Sometimes, it will not be profitable for a unit to become engaged in a certain area, and in that case, it must move immediately.

When the situation is serious, the guerrilla must move with the fluidity of water and the ease of the blowing wind. Their tactics must deceive, tempt, and confuse the enemy. They must lead the enemy to believe that they will attack him from the east and north, and they must then strike him from the west and the south. They must strike, then rapidly disperse. They must move at night.

Guerrilla initiative is expressed in dispersion, concentration, and the alert shifting of forces. If guerrillas are stupid and obstinate, they will be led to passive positions and severely damaged. Skill in conducting guerrilla operations, however, lies not in merely understanding the things we have discussed but rather in their actual application on the field of battle. The quick intelligence that constantly watches the ever-changing situation and is able to seize on the right moment for decisive action is found only in keen and thoughtful observers.

Mao Zedong

Careful planning is necessary if victory is to be won in guerrilla war, and those who fight without method do not understand the nature of guerrilla action. A plan is necessary regardless of the size of the unit involved; a prudent plan is as necessary in the case of the squad as in the case of the regiment. The situation must be carefully studied, then an assignment of duties made. Plans must include both political and military instruction; the matter of supply and equipment, and the matter of co-operation with local civilians. Without study of these factors, it is impossible either to seize the initiative or to operate alertly. It is true that guerrillas can make only limited plans, but even so, the factors we have mentioned must be considered.

The initiative can be secured and retained only following a positive victory that results from attack. The attack must be made on guerrilla initiative; that is, guerrillas must not permit themselves to be maneuvered into a position where they are robbed of initiative and where the decision to attack is forced upon them. Any victory will result from careful planning and alert control. Even in defense, all our efforts must be directed toward a resumption of the attack, for it is only by attack that we can extinguish our enemies and preserve ourselves. A defense or a withdrawal is entirely useless as far as extinguishing our enemies is concerned and of only temporary value, as far as the conservation of our forces is concerned. This principle is valid both for guerrillas and regular troops. The differences are of degree only; that is to say, in the manner of execution.

The relationship that exists between guerrilla and the orthodox forces is important and must be appreciated. Generally speaking, there are types of co-operation between guerrillas and orthodox groups. These are:

1. Strategic co-operation
2. Tactical co-operation
3. Battle co-operation

Guerrillas who harass the enemy's rear installations and hinder his transport are weakening him and encouraging the national spirit of resistance. They are co-operating strategically. For example, the guerrillas in Manchuria had no functions of strategic co-operation with orthodox forces until the war in China started. Since that time, their faction of strategic co-operation is evident, for if they can kill one enemy, make the enemy expend one round of ammunition, or hinder one enemy group in its advance southward, our powers of resistance here are proportionately increased. Such guerrilla action has a positive action on the enemy nation and on its troops, while, at the same time, it encourages our own countrymen. Another example of strategic co-operation is furnished by the guerrillas who operate along the P'ing-Sui, P'ing-Han, Chin-P'u, T'ung-Pu, and Cheng-T'ai railways. This co-operation began when the invader attacked, continued during the period when he held garrisoned cities in the areas, and was intensified when our regular forces counter-attacked, in an effort to restore the lost territories.

As an example of tactical co-operation, we may cite the operations at Hsing-K'ou, when guerrillas both north and south of Yeh Men destroyed the T'ung-P'u railway and the motor roads near P'ing Hosing Pass and Yang Fang K'ou. A number of small operating base were established, and organized guerrilla action in Shansi complemented the activities of the regular forces both there and in the defense of Honan. similarly, during the south Shantung campaign, guerrillas in the five northern provinces co-operated with the army's operation on the Hsuchow front.

Guerrilla commanders in rear areas and those in command of regiments assigned to operate with orthodox units must co-operate in accordance with the situation. It is their function to determine weak points in the enemy dispositions, harass them, to disrupt their transport, and to undermine their morale, If guerrilla action were independent, the results to be obtained from tactical co-operation would be lost and those that result from strategic co-operation greatly diminished. In order to accomplish their mission and improve the degree of co-operation, guerrilla units must be equipped with some means of rapid communication. For this purpose, two way radio sets are recommended.

Guerrilla forces in the immediate battle area are responsible for close co-operation with regular forces, Their principal functions are to hinder enemy transport to gather information, and to act as outposts and sentinels. Even without precise instructions from the commander of the regular forces, these missions, as well as any others that contribute to the general success, should be assumed.

The problem of establishment of bases is of particular importance. This is so because this war is a cruel and protracted struggle. The lost territories can be restored only by a strategic counter-attack and this we cannot carry out until the enemy is well into China. Consequently, some part of our country — or, indeed, most of it — may be captured by the enemy and become his rear area. It is our task to develop intensive guerrilla warfare over this vast area and convert the enemy's rear into an additional front. Thus the enemy will never be able to stop fighting. In order to subdue the occupied territory, the enemy will have to become increasingly severe and oppressive.

A guerrilla base may be defined as an area, strategically located, in which the guerrillas can carry out their duties of training, self-preservation and development. Ability to fight a war without a rear area is a fundamental characteristic of guerrilla action, but this does not mean that guerrilla can exist and function over a long period of time without the development of base areas. History shows us many examples of peasant revolts that were unsuccessful, and it is fanciful to believe that such movements, characterized by banditry and brigandage, could succeed in this era of improved communications and military equipment. Some guerrilla leaders seem to think that those qualities are present in today's movement, and before such leaders can comprehend the importance of base areas in the long-term war, their mind must be disabused of this idea.

The subject of bases may be better understood if we consider:

1.   The various categories of bases
2.   Guerrilla areas and base areas
3.   The establishment of bases
4.   The development of bases

Guerrilla bases may be classified according to their location as: first, mountain bases; second, plains bases; and last, river, lake, and bay bases. The advantages of bases in mountainous areas are evident. Those which are now established are at Ch'ang P'o Chan, Wu Tai Shan, Taiheng Shan, Tai Shan, Yen Shan, and Mao Shan. These bases are strongly protected. Similar bases should be established in all enemy rear areas.

Plains country is generally not satisfactory for guerrilla operating bases, but this does not mean that guerrilla warfare cannot flourish in such country or that bases cannot be established there. The extent of guerrilla development in Hopeh and west Shantung proves the opposite to be the case. Whether we can count on the use of these bases over long periods of time is questionable. We can, however, establish small bases of a seasonal or temporary nature. This we can do because our barbaric enemy simply does not have the manpower to occupy all the areas he has overrun and because the population of China is so numerous that a base can be established anywhere. Seasonal bases in plains country may be established in the winter when the rivers are frozen over, and in the summer when the crops are growing. Temporary bases may be established when the enemy is otherwise occupied. When the enemy advances, the guerrillas who have established bases in the plains area are the first to engage him. Upon their withdrawal into mountainous country, they should leave behind them guerrilla groups dispersed over the entire area. Guerrillas shift from base to base on the theory that they must be in one place one day and another place the next.

There are many historical examples of the establishment of bases in river, bay, and lake country, and this is one aspect of our activity that has so far received little attention. Red guerrillas held out for many years in the Hungtze Lake region. We should establish bases in the Hungtze and Tai areas and along rivers and watercourses in territory controlled by the enemy so as to deny him access to, and free use of, the water routes.

There is a difference between the terms base area and guerrilla area. An area completely surrounded by territory occupied by the enemy is a 'base area'. Wu Tai Shan, and Taiheng Shan are examples of base areas. On the other hand, the area east and north of Wu Tai Shan (the Shansi-Hopeh-Chahar border zone) is a guerrilla area. Such areas can be controlled by guerrillas only while they actually physically occupy them. Upon their departure, control reverts to a puppet pro-Japanese government. East Hopeh, for example, was at first a guerrilla area rather than a base area. A puppet government functioned there. Eventually, the people, organized and inspired by guerrillas from the Wu Tai mountains, assisted in the transformation of this guerrilla area into a real base area. Such a task is extremely difficult, for it is largely dependent upon the degree to which the people can be inspired. In certain garrisoned areas, such as the cities and zones contiguous to the railways, the guerrillas see unable to drive the Japanese and puppets out. These areas remain guerrilla areas. At other times, base areas might become guerrilla areas due either to our own mistakes or to the activities of the enemy.

Obviously, in any given area in the war zone, any one or three situations may develop: The area may remain in Chinese hands; it may be lost to the Japanese and puppets or it may be divided between the combatants. Guerrilla leaders should endeavor to see that either the first or the last of these situations is assured.

Another point essential in the establishment of bases is the co-operation that must exist between the armed guerrilla bands and the people. All our strength must be used to spread the doctrine of armed resistance to Japan, to arm the people, to organize self-defense units, and to train guerrilla bands. This doctrine must be spread among the people, who must be organized into anti-Japanese groups. Their political instincts must be sharpened and their martial ardor increased. If the workers, the farmers, the lovers of liberty, the young men, the women, and the children are not organized, they will never realize their own anti-Japanese power. Only the united strength of the people can eliminate traitors, recover the measure of political power that has been lost, and conserve and improve what we still retain.

We have already touched on geographic factors in our discussion of bases, and we must also mention the economic aspects of the problem. What economic policy should be adopted? Any such policy must offer reasonable protection to commerce and business. We interpret 'reasonable protection' to mean the people must contribute money in proportion to the money they have. Farmers will be required to furnish a certain share of their crops to guerrilla troops. Confiscation, except in the case of business run by traitors, is prohibited.

Our activities must be extended over the entire periphery of the base area if we wish to attack the enemy's bases and thus strengthen and develop our own. This will afford us opportunity to organize, equip, and train the people, thus furthering guerrilla policy as well as the national policy of protected war. At times, we must emphasize the development and extension of base areas; at other times, the organization, training, or equipment of the people.

Each guerrilla base will have its own peculiar problems of attack and defense. In general, the enemy, in an endeavor to consolidate his gains, will attempt to extinguish guerrilla bases by dispatching numerous bodies of troops over a number of different routes. This must be anticipated and the encirclement broken by counter-attacks As such enemy columns are without reserves, we should plan on using our main forces to attack one of them by surprise and devote our secondary effort to continual hindrance and harassment. At the same time, other forces should isolate enemy garrison troops and operate on their lines of supply and communication. When one column has been disposed of, we may turn our attention to one of the others. In a base area as large as Wu Tat Shan, for example, there are four or five military sub-divisions. Guerrillas in these sub-divisions must co-operate to form a primary force to counterattack the enemy, or the area from which he came, while a secondary force harasses and hinders him.

After defeating the enemy in any area, we must take advantage of the period he requires for reorganization to press home our attacks. We must not attack an objective we are not certain of winning. We must confine our operations to relatively small areas and destroy the enemy and traitors in those places.

When the inhabitants have been inspired, new volunteers accepted trained, equipped, and organized, our operations may be extended to include cities and lines of communication not strongly held. We may hold these at least for temporary (if not permanent) periods. All these are our duties in offensive strategy. Their object is to lengthen the period that the enemy must remain on the defensive. Then our military activities and our organization work among the masses of the people must be zealously expanded; and with equal zeal, the strength of the enemy attacked and diminished. It is of great importance that guerrilla units be rested and instructed. During such times as the enemy is on the defensive, the troops may get some rest and instruction may be carried out.

The development of mobile warfare is not only possible but essential. This is the case because our current war is a desperate and protracted struggle. If China were able to conquer the Japanese bandits speedily and to recover her lost territories, there would be no question of long-term war on a national scale. Hence there would no question of the relation of guerrilla hostilities into mobile warfare of an orthodox nature; both the quantity and quality of guerrilla must be improved. Primarily, more men must join the armies; then the quality of equipment and standards of training must be improved. Political training must be emphasized and our organization, the technique of handling our weapons, our tactics — all must be improved. Our internal discipline must be strengthened. The soldiers must be educated politically. There must be a gradual change from guerrilla formations to orthodox regimental organization. The necessary bureaus and staffs, both political and military, must be provided. At the same time, attention must be paid to the creation of suitable supply, medical, and hygiene units. The standards of equipment must be raised and types of weapons increased. Communication equipment must not be forgotten. Orthodox standards of discipline must be established.

Because guerrilla formations act independently and because they are the most elementary of armed formations, command cannot be too highly centralized. If it were, guerilla action would be too limited in scope. At the same time, guerrilla activities, to be most effective, must be co-ordinated, not only in so far as they themselves are concerned, but additionally with regular troops operating in the same areas. This co-ordination is a function of the war zone commander and his staff.

In guerrilla base areas, the command must be centralized for strategic purposes and decentralized for tactical purposes. Centralized strategic command takes care of the general management of all guerrilla units, their co-ordination within war zones, and the general policy regarding guerrilla base areas. Beyond this, centralization of command will result in interference with subordinate units, as, naturally, the tactics to apply to concrete situations can be determined only as these various situations arise. This is true in orthodox warfare when communications between lower and higher echelons break down. In a word, proper guerrilla policy will provide for unified strategy and independent activity.

Each guerrilla area is divided into districts and these in turn are divided into sub-districts. Each sub-division has its appointed commander, and while general plans are made by higher commanders, the nature of actions is determined by inferior commanders. The former may suggest the nature of the action to be taken but cannot define it. Thus inferior groups heave more or less complete local control.

THE RED BOOK
OF
GUERRILLA WARFARE

PART 2

PROBLEMS OF STRATEGY
IN GUERRILLA WAR
AGAINST JAPAN

Preface

May, 1938

In the early days of the War of Resistance against Japan, many people inside and outside the Party belittled the important strategic role of guerrilla warfare and pinned their hopes on regular warfare alone, and particularly on the operations of the Kuomintang forces. Comrade Mao Zedong refuted this view and wrote this article to show the correct road of development for anti-Japanese guerrilla warfare.

As a result, the Eighth Route Army and the New Fourth Army, which had just over 40,000 men when the War of Resistance began in 1937, grew to a great army of one million by the time Japan surrendered in 1945, established many revolutionary base areas, played a great part in the war and thus, throughout this period, made Chiang Kai-shek afraid to capitulate to Japan or launch a nation-wide civil war.

In 1946, when Chiang Kai-shek did launch a nation-wide civil war, the People's Liberation Army, formed out of the Eighth Route and New Fourth Armies, was strong enough to deal with his attacks.

CHAPTER 1

Why Raise the Question of Strategy?

In the War of Resistance against Japan, regular warfare is primary and guerrilla warfare supplementary. This point has already been correctly settled. Thus, it seems there are only tactical problems in guerrilla warfare. Why then raise the question of strategy?

If China were a small country in which the role of guerrilla warfare was only to render direct support over short distances to the campaigns of the regular army, there would, of course, be only tactical problems but no strategic ones. On the other hand, if China were a country as strong as the Soviet Union and the invading enemy could either be quickly expelled, or, even though his expulsion were to take some time, he could not occupy extensive areas, then again guerrilla warfare would simply play a supporting role in campaigns, and would naturally involve only tactical but not strategic problems.

The question of strategy in guerrilla war does arise, however, in the case of China, which is neither small nor like the Soviet Union, but which is both a large and a weak country. This large and weak country is being attacked by a small and strong country, but the large and weak country is in an era of progress; this is the source of the whole problem. It is in these circumstances that vast areas have come under enemy occupation and that the war has become a protracted one. The enemy is occupying vast areas of this large country of ours, but Japan is a small country, she does not have sufficient soldiers and has to leave many gaps in the occupied areas, so that our anti Japanese guerrilla warfare consists primarily not in interior-line operations in support of the campaigns of the regular troops but in independent operations on exterior lines; furthermore, China is progressive, that is to say, she has a staunch army and broad masses of people, both led by the Communist Party, so that, far from being small-scale, our anti-Japanese guerrilla warfare is in fact large-scale warfare. Hence the emergence of a whole series of problems, such as the strategic defensive, the strategic offensive, etc. The protracted nature of the war and its attendant ruthlessness have made it imperative for guerrilla warfare to undertake many unusual tasks; hence such problems as those of the base areas, the development of guerrilla warfare into mobile warfare, and so on. For all these reasons, China's guerrilla warfare against Japan has broken out of the bounds of tactics to knock at the gates of strategy, and it demands examination from the viewpoint of strategy. The point that merits our particular attention is that such extensive as well as protracted guerrilla warfare is quite new in the entire history of war. This is bound up with the fact that we are now in the Nineteen Thirties and Nineteen Forties and that we now have the Communist Party and the Red Army. Herein lies the heart of the matter. Our enemy is probably still cherishing fond dreams of emulating the Mongol conquest of the Sung Dynasty, the Manchu conquest of the Ming Dynasty, the British occupation of North America and India, the Latin occupation of Central and South America, etc. But such dreams have no practical value in present-day China because there are certain factors present in the China of today which were absent in those historical instances, and one of them is guerrilla warfare, which is quite a new phenomenon. If our enemy overlooks this fact, he will certainly come to grief.

These are the reasons why our anti-Japanese guerrilla warfare, though occupying only a supplementary place in the

War of Resistance as a whole, must nevertheless be examined from the viewpoint of strategy.

Why not, then, apply to guerrilla warfare the general strategic principles of the War of Resistance?

The question of strategy in our anti-Japanese guerrilla warfare is indeed closely linked with the question of strategy in the War of Resistance as a whole, because they have much in common. On the other hand, guerrilla warfare is different from regular warfare and has its own peculiarities, and consequently many peculiar elements are involved in the question of strategy in guerrilla warfare. With out modification it is impossible to apply the strategic principles of the War of Resistance in general to guerrilla warfare with its own peculiarities.

CHAPTER 2

The Basic Principle of War is to Preserve Oneself and Destroy the Enemy

Before discussing the question of strategy in guerrilla warfare in concrete terms, a few words are needed on the fundamental problem of war. All the guiding principles of military operations grow out of the one basic principle: to strive to the utmost to preserve one's own strength and destroy that of the enemy. In a revolutionary war, this principle is directly linked with basic political principles. For instance, the basic political principle of China's War of Resistance against Japan, i.e., its political aim, is to drive out Japanese imperialism and build an independent, free and happy new China.

In terms of military action this principle means the use of armed force to defend our motherland and to drive out the Japanese invaders. To attain this end, the operations of the armed units take the form of doing their utmost to preserve their own strength on the one hand and destroy the enemy's on the other. How then do we justify the encouragement of heroic sacrifice in war? Every war exacts a price, sometimes an extremely high one. Is this not in contradiction with "preserving oneself"? In fact, there is no contradiction at all; to put it more exactly, sacrifice and self-preservation are both opposite and complementary to each other. For such sacrifice is essential not only for destroying the enemy but also for preserving oneself -- partial and temporary "non-preservation" (sacrifice, or paying the price) is necessary for the sake of general and permanent preservation. From this basic principle stems the series of principles guiding military operations, all of which -- from the principles of shooting (taking cover to preserve oneself, and making full use of fire-power to destroy the enemy) to the principles of strategy -- are permeated with the spirit of this basic principle. All technical, tactical and strategic principles represent applications of this basic principle. The principle of preserving one self and destroying the enemy is the basis of all military principles.

CHAPTER 3

Six Specific Problems of Strategy in Guerrilla War against Japan

Now let us see what policies or principles have to be adopted in guerrilla operations against Japan before we can attain the object of preserving ourselves and destroying the enemy. Since the guerrilla units in the War of Resistance (and in all other revolutionary wars) generally grow out of nothing and expand from a small to a large force, they must preserve themselves and, moreover, they must expand. Hence the question is, what policies or principles have to be adopted before we can attain the object of preserving and expanding ourselves and destroying the enemy?

Generally speaking, the main principles are as follows: (1) the use of initiative, flexibility and planning in conducting offensives within the defensive, battles of quick decision within protracted war, and exterior-line operations within interior-line operations; (2) co-ordination with regular warfare; (3) establishment of base areas; (4) the strategic defensive and the strategic offensive; (5) the development of guerrilla warfare into mobile warfare; and (6) correct relationship of command. These six items constitute the whole of the strategic program for guerrilla war against Japan and are the means necessary for the preservation and expansion of our forces, for the destruction and expulsion of the enemy, for co-ordination with regular warfare and the winning of final victory.

CHAPTER 4

Initiative, Flexibility and Planning in Conducting Offensives within the Defensive Battles of Quick Decision within Protracted War, and Exterior-Line Operations within Interior-Line Operations

Here the subject may be dealt with under four headings: (1) the relationship between the defensive and the offensive, between protractedness and quick decision, and between the interior and exterior lines; (2) the initiative in all operations; (3) flexible employment of forces; and (4) planning in all operations.

To start with the first.

If we take the War of Resistance as a whole, the fact that Japan is a strong country and is attacking while China is a weak country and is defending herself makes our war strategically a defensive and protracted war. As far as the operational lines are concerned, the Japanese are operating on exterior and we on interior lines. This is one aspect of the situation. But there is another aspect which is just the reverse. The enemy forces, though strong (in arms, in certain qualities of their men, and certain other factors), are numerically small, whereas our forces, though weak (likewise, in arms, in certain qualities of our men, and certain other factors), are numerically very large. Added to the fact that the enemy is an alien nation invading our country while we are resisting his invasion on our own soil, this determines the following strategy. It is possible and necessary to use tactical offensives within the strategic defensive, to fight campaigns and battles of quick decision within a strategically protracted war and to fight campaigns and battles on exterior lines within strategically interior lines. Such is the strategy to be adopted in the War of Resistance as a whole. It holds true both for regular and for guerrilla warfare. Guerrilla warfare is different only in degree and form. Offensives in guerrilla warfare generally take the form of surprise attacks. Although surprise attacks can and should be employed in regular warfare too, the degree of surprise is less. In guerrilla warfare, the need to bring operations to a quick decision is very great, and our exterior-line ring of encirclement of the enemy in campaigns and battles is very small All these distinguish it from regular warfare.

Thus it can be seen that in their operations guerrilla units have to concentrate the maximum forces, act secretly and swiftly, attack the enemy by surprise and bring battles to a quick decision, and that they must strictly avoid passive defense, procrastination and the dispersal of forces before engagements. Of course, guerrilla warfare includes not only the strategic but also the tactical defensive. The latter embraces, among other things, containing and outpost actions during battles; the disposition of forces for resistance at narrow passes, strategic points, rivers or villages in order to deplete and exhaust the enemy; and action to cover withdrawal. But the basic principle of guerrilla warfare must be the offensive, and guerrilla warfare is more offensive in its character than regular warfare. The offensive, moreover, must take the form of surprise attacks, and to expose our selves by ostentatiously parading our forces is even less permissible in guerrilla warfare than in regular warfare. From the fact that the enemy is strong and we are weak it necessarily follows that, in guerrilla operations in general even more than in regular warfare, battles must be decided quickly, though on some occasions guerrilla fighting may be kept up for several days, as in an assault on a small and isolated enemy force cut off from help. Because of

Mao Zedong

its dispersed character, guerrilla warfare can spread everywhere, and in many of its tasks, as in harassing, containing and disrupting the enemy and in mass work, its principle is dispersal of forces; but a guerrilla unit, or a guerrilla formation, must concentrate its main forces when it is engaged in destroying the enemy, and especially when it is striving to smash an enemy attack. "Concentrate a big force to strike at a small section of the enemy force" remains a principle of field operations in guerrilla warfare.

Thus it can also be seen that, if we take the War of Resistance as a whole, we can attain the aim of our strategic defensive and finally defeat Japanese imperialism only through the cumulative effect of many offensive campaigns and battles in both regular and guerrilla warfare, namely, through the cumulative effect of many victories in offensive actions. Only through the cumulative effect of many campaigns and battles of quick decision, namely, the cumulative effect of many victories achieved through quick decision in offensive campaigns and battles, can we attain our goal of strategic protractedness, which means gaining time to increase our capacity to resist while hastening or awaiting changes in the international situation and the internal collapse of the enemy, in order to be able to launch a strategic counter-offensive and drive the Japanese invaders out of China. We must concentrate superior forces and fight exterior-line operations in every campaign or battle, whether in the stage of strategic defensive or in that of strategic counter-offensive, in order to encircle and destroy the enemy forces, encircling part if not all of them, destroying part if not all of the forces we have encircled, and inflicting heavy casualties on the encircled forces if we cannot capture them in large numbers. Only through the cumulative effect of many such battles of annihilation can we change the relative position as between the enemy and ourselves, thoroughly smash his strategic encirclement -- that is, his scheme of exterior-line operations -- and finally, in co-ordination with international forces and the revolutionary struggles of the Japanese people, surround the Japanese imperialists and deal them the coup de grace. These results are to be achieved mainly through regular warfare, with guerrilla warfare making a secondary contribution. What is common to both, however, is the accumulation of many minor victories to make a major victory. Herein lies the great strategic role of guerrilla warfare in the War of Resistance.

Now let us discuss initiative, flexibility and planning in guerrilla warfare.

What is initiative in guerrilla warfare?

In any war, the opponents contend for the initiative, whether on a battlefield, in a battle area, in a war zone or in the whole war, for the initiative means freedom of action for an army. Any army which, losing the initiative, is forced into a passive position and ceases to have freedom of action, faces the danger of defeat or extermination. Naturally, gaining the initiative is harder in strategic defensive and interior-line operations and easier in offensive exterior-line operations. However, Japanese imperialism has two basic weaknesses, namely, its shortage of troops and the fact that it is fighting on foreign soil. Moreover, its underestimation of China's strength and the internal contradictions among the Japanese militarists have given rise to many mistakes in command, such as piecemeal reinforcement, lack of strategic co-ordination, occasional absence of a main direction for attack, failure to grasp opportunities in some operations and failure to wipe out encircled forces, all of which may be considered the third weakness of Japanese imperialism. Thus, despite the advantage of being on the offensive and operating on exterior lines, the Japanese militarists are gradually losing the initiative, because of their shortage of troops (their small territory, small population, inadequate resources, feudalistic imperialism, etc.), because of the fact that they are fighting on foreign soil (their war is imperialist and barbarous) and because of their stupidities in command. Japan is neither willing nor able to conclude the war at present, nor has her strategic offensive yet come to an end, but, as the general trend shows, her offensive is confined within certain limits, which is the inevitable consequence of her three weaknesses; she cannot go on indefinitely till she swallows the whole of China. Already there are signs that Japan will one day find herself in an utterly passive position. China, on the other hand, was in a rather passive position at the beginning of the war, but, having gained experience, she is now turning to the new policy of mobile warfare, the policy of taking the offensive, seeking quick decisions and operating on exterior lines in campaigns and battles, which, together with the policy of developing widespread guerrilla warfare, is helping China to build up a position of initiative day by day.

The question of the initiative is even more vital in guerrilla warfare. For most guerrilla units operate in very difficult circumstances, fighting without a rear, with their own weak forces facing the enemy's strong forces, lacking experience (when the units are newly organized), being separated, etc. Nevertheless, it is possible to build up the initiative in guerrilla warfare, the essential condition being to seize on the enemy's three weaknesses. Taking advantage of the enemy's shortage of troops (from the viewpoint of the war as a whole), the guerrilla units can boldly use vast areas as their fields of operation; taking advantage of the fact that the enemy is an alien invader and is pursuing a most barbarous policy, the guerrilla units can boldly enlist the support of millions upon millions of people; and taking advantage of the stupidities in the enemy's command, the guerrilla units can give full scope to their resourcefulness. While the regular army must seize on all these weaknesses of the enemy and turn them to good account in order to defeat him, it is even more important for the guerrilla units to do so. As for the guerrilla units' own weaknesses, they can be gradually reduced in the course of the struggle. Moreover, these weaknesses sometimes constitute the very condition for gaining the initiative. For example, it is precisely because the guerrilla units are small that they can mysteriously appear and disappear in their operations behind enemy lines, without the enemy's being able to do anything about them, and thus enjoy a freedom of action such as massive regular armies never can.

When the enemy is making a converging attack from several directions, a guerrilla unit can exercise initiative only with difficulty and can lose it all too easily. In such a case, if its appraisals and dispositions are wrong, it is liable to get into a passive position and consequently fail to smash the converging enemy attack. This may occur even when the enemy is on the defensive and we are on the offensive. For the initiative results from making a correct appraisal of the situation (both our own and that of the enemy) and from making the correct military and political dispositions. A pessimistic appraisal out of accord with the objective conditions and the passive dispositions ensuing from it will undoubtedly result in the loss of the initiative and throw one into a passive position. On the other hand, an over-optimistic appraisal out of accord with the objective conditions and the risky (unjustifiably risky) dispositions ensuing from it will also result in the loss of the initiative and eventually land one in a position similar to that of the pessimists. The initiative is not an innate attribute of genius, but is something an intelligent leader attains through open-minded study and correct appraisal of the objective conditions and through correct military and political dispositions. It follows that the initiative is not ready-made but is something that requires conscious effort.

Mao Zedong

When forced into a passive position through some incorrect appraisal and disposition or through overwhelming pressure, a guerrilla unit must strive to extricate itself. How this can be done depends on the circumstances. In many cases it is necessary to "move away". The ability to move is the distinctive feature of a guerrilla unit. To move away is the principal method for getting out of a passive position and regaining the initiative. But it is not the sole method. The moment when the enemy is most energetic and we are in the greatest difficulties is often the very moment when things begin to turn against him and in our favor. Frequently a favorable situation recurs and the initiative is regained as a result of "holding out a little longer".

Next, let us deal with flexibility.

Flexibility is a concrete expression of the initiative. The flexible employment of forces is more essential in guerrilla warfare than in regular warfare.

A guerrilla commander must understand that the flexible employment of his forces is the most important means of changing the situation as between the enemy and ourselves and of gaining the initiative. The nature of guerrilla warfare is such that guerrilla forces must be employed flexibly in accordance with the task in hand and with such circumstances as the state of the enemy, the terrain and the local population, and the chief ways of employing the forces are dispersal, concentration and shifting of position. In employing his forces, a guerrilla commander is like a fisherman casting his net, which he should be able to spread wide as well as draw in tight. When casting his net, the fisherman has to ascertain the depth of the water, the speed of the current and the presence or absence of obstructions; similarly, when dispersing his units, a guerrilla commander must take care not to incur losses through ignorance of the situation or through miscalculated action. Just as the fisherman must keep a grip on the cord in order to draw his net in tight, so the guerrilla commander must maintain liaison and communication with all his forces and keep enough of his main forces at hand. Just as a frequent change of position is necessary in fishing, so a frequent shift of position is necessary for a guerrilla unit. Dispersal, concentration and shifting of position are the three ways of flexibly employing forces in guerrilla warfare. Generally speaking, the dispersal of guerrilla units, or "breaking up the whole into parts", is employed chiefly: (1) when we want to threaten the enemy with a wide frontal attack because he is on the defensive, and there is temporarily no chance to mass our forces for action; (2) when we want to harass and disrupt the enemy throughout an area where his forces are weak; (3) when we are unable to break through the enemy's encirclement and try to slip away by making ourselves less conspicuous; (4) when we are restricted by terrain or supplies; or (5) when we are carrying on mass work over a wide area. But whatever the circumstances, when dispersing for action we should pay attention to the following: 1) we should never make an absolutely even dispersal of forces, but should keep a fairly large part in an area convenient for maneuver, so that any possible exigency can be met and there is a centre of gravity for the task being carried out in dispersion; and (2) we should assign to the dispersed units clearly defined tasks, fields of operation, time limits for actions, places for reassembly and ways and means of liaison.

Concentration of forces, or "assembling the parts into a whole", is the method usually applied to destroy an enemy when he is on the offensive and sometimes to destroy some of his stationary forces when he is on the defensive. Concentration of forces does not mean absolute concentration, but the massing of the main forces for use in one important direction while retaining or dispatching part of the forces for use in other directions to contain, harass or disrupt the enemy, or to carry on mass work.

Although the flexible dispersal or concentration of forces according to circumstances is the principal method in guerrilla warfare, we must also know how to shift (or transfer) our forces flexibly. When the enemy feels seriously threatened by guerrillas, he will send troops to attack or suppress them. Hence the guerrilla units will have to take stock of the situation. If advisable, they should fight where they are; if not, they should lose no time in shifting elsewhere. Sometimes, in order to crush the enemy units one by one, guerrilla units which have destroyed an enemy force in one place may immediately shift to another so as to wipe out a second enemy force; sometimes, finding it inadvisable to fight in one place, they may have to disengage quickly and fight the enemy elsewhere. If the enemy's forces in a certain place present a particularly serious threat, the guerrilla units should not linger, but should move off with lightning speed. In general, shifts of position should be made with secrecy and speed. In order to mislead, decoy and confuse the enemy, they should constantly use stratagems, such as making a feint to the east but attacking in the west, appearing now in the south and now in the north, hit-and-run attacks, and night actions.

Flexibility in dispersal, concentration and shifts of position is a concrete expression of the initiative in guerrilla warfare, whereas rigidness and inertia inevitably lead to passivity and cause unnecessary losses. But a commander proves himself wise not just by recognition of the importance of employing his forces flexibly but by skill in dispersing, concentrating or shifting them in good time according to the specific circumstances. This wisdom in sensing changes and choosing the right moment to act is not easily acquired; it can be gained only by those who study with a receptive mind and investigate and ponder diligently. Prudent consideration of the circumstances is essential to prevent flexibility from turning into impulsive action.

Lastly, we come to planning.

Without planning, victories in guerrilla warfare are impossible. Any idea that guerrilla warfare can be conducted in haphazard fashion indicates either a flippant attitude or ignorance of guerrilla warfare. The operations in a guerrilla zone as a whole, or those of a guerrilla unit or formation, must be preceded by as thorough planning as possible, by preparation in advance for every action. Grasping the situation, setting the tasks, disposing the forces, giving military and political training, securing supplies, putting the equipment in good order, making proper use of the people's help, etc. -- all these are part of the work of the guerrilla commanders, which they must carefully consider and conscientiously perform and check up on. There can be no initiative, no flexibility, and no offensive unless they do so. True, guerrilla conditions do not allow as high a degree of planning as do those of regular warfare, and it would be a mistake to attempt very thorough planning in guerrilla warfare. But it is necessary to plan as thoroughly as the objective conditions permit, for it should be understood that fighting the enemy is no joke.

The above points serve to explain the first of the strategic principles of guerrilla warfare, the principle of using initiative, flexibility and planning in conducting offensives within the defensive, battles of quick decision within protracted war, and exterior-line operations within interior-line operations. It is the key problem in the strategy of guerrilla warfare. The solution of this problem provides the major guarantee of victory in guerrilla warfare so far as military command is concerned.

Although a variety of matters have been dealt with here, they all revolve around the offensive in campaigns and battles. The initiative can be decisively grasped only after victory in an offensive. Every offensive operation must be organized on our initiative and not launched under compulsion. Flexibility in the employment of forces revolves around the effort to take the offensive, and planning likewise is necessary chiefly in order to ensure success in offensive operations. Measures of tactical defense are meaningless if they are divorced from their role of giving either direct or indirect support to an offensive. Ouick decision refers to the tempo of an offensive, and exterior lines refer to its scope. The offensive is the only means of destroying the enemy and is also the principal means of self-preservation, while pure defense and retreat can play only a temporary and partial role in self-preservation and are quite useless for destroying the enemy.

The principle stated above is basically the same for both regular and guerrilla war; it differs to some degree only in its form of expression. But in guerrilla war it is both important and necessary to note this difference. It is precisely this difference in form which distinguishes the operational methods of guerrilla war from those of regular war. If we confuse the two different forms in which the principle is expressed, victory in guerrilla war will be impossible.

Chapter 5

Co-ordination with Regular Warfare

The second problem of strategy in guerrilla warfare is its co-ordination with regular warfare. It is a matter of clarifying the relation between guerrilla and regular warfare on the operational level, in the light of the nature of actual guerrilla operations. An understanding of this relation is very important for effectiveness in defeating the enemy.

There are three kinds of co-ordination between guerrilla and regular warfare, co-ordination in strategy, in campaigns and in battles.

Taken as a whole, guerrilla warfare behind the enemy lines, which cripples the enemy, pins him down, disrupts his supply lines and inspires the regular forces and the people throughout the country, is co-ordinated with regular warfare in strategy. Take the case of the guerrilla warfare in the three northeastern provinces. Of course, the question of co-ordination did not arise before the nation-wide War of Resistance, but since the war began the significance of such co-ordination has become obvious. Every enemy soldier the guerrillas kill there, every bullet they make the enemy expend, every enemy soldier they stop from advancing south of the Great Wall, can be reckoned a contribution to the total strength of the resistance. It is, moreover, clear that they are having a demoralizing effect on the whole enemy army and all Japan and a heartening effect on our whole army and people. Still clearer is the role in strategic co-ordination played by the guerrilla warfare along the Peiping-Suiyuan, Peiping-Hankow, Tientsin-Pukow, Tatung-Puchow, Chengting-Taiyuan and Shanghai-Hangchow

Railways. Not only are the guerrilla units performing the function of co-ordination with the regular forces in our present strategic defensive, when the enemy is on the strategic offensive; not only will they co-ordinate with the regular forces in disrupting the enemy's hold on the occupied territory, after he concludes his strategic offensive and switches to the safeguarding of his gains; they will also co-ordinate with the regular forces in driving out the enemy forces and recovering all the lost territories, when the regular forces launch the strategic counter-offensive. The great role of guerrilla warfare in strategic co-ordination must not be overlooked. The commanders both of the guerrilla units and of the regular forces must clearly understand this role.

In addition, guerrilla warfare performs the function of co-ordination with regular warfare in campaigns. For instance, in the campaign at Hsinkou, north of Taiyuan, the guerrillas played a remarkable role in co-ordination both north and south of Yenmenkuan by wrecking the Tatung-Puchow Railway and the motor roads running through Pinghsingkuan and Yangfangkou. Or take another instance. After the enemy occupied Fenglingtu, guerrilla warfare, which was already widespread throughout Shansi Province and was conducted mainly by the regular forces, played an even greater role through co-ordination with the defensive campaigns west of the Yellow River in Shensi Province and south of the Yellow River in Honan Province. Again, when the enemy attacked southern Shantung, the guerrilla warfare in the five provinces of northern China contributed a great deal through co-ordination with the campaigns of our army. In performing a task of this sort, the leaders of each guerrilla base behind the enemy lines, or the commanders of a guerrilla formation temporarily dispatched there, must dispose their forces well and, by adopting different tactics suited to the time and place, move energetically against the enemy's most vital and vulnerable spots in order to cripple him, pin him down, disrupt his supply lines, inspire our armies campaigning on the interior lines, and so fulfill their duty of co-ordinating with the campaign. If each guerrilla zone or unit goes it alone without giving any attention to co-ordinating with the campaigns of the regular forces, its role in strategic co-ordination will lose a great deal of its significance, although it will still play some such role in the general strategy. All guerrilla commanders should give this point serious attention. To achieve co-ordination in campaigns, it is absolutely necessary for all larger guerrilla units and guerrilla formations to have radio equipment.

Finally, co-ordination with the regular forces in battles, in actual fighting on the battlefield, is the task of all guerrilla units in the vicinity of an interior-line battlefield. Of course, this applies only to guerrilla units operating close to the regular forces or to units of regulars dispatched on temporary guerrilla missions. In such cases, a guerrilla unit has to perform whatever task it is assigned by the commander of the regular forces, which is usually to pin down some of the enemy's forces, disrupt his supply lines, conduct reconnaissance, or act as guides for the regular forces. Even without such an assignment, the guerrilla unit should carry out these tasks on its own initiative. To sit by idly, neither moving nor fighting, or to move about without fighting, would be an intolerable attitude for a guerrilla unit.

Chapter 6

The Establishment of the Base Area

The third problem of strategy in anti-Japanese guerrilla warfare is the establishment of base areas, which is important and essential because of the protracted nature and ruthlessness of the war. The recovery of our lost territories will have to await the nation-wide strategic counter-offensive; by then the enemy's front will have extended deep into central China and cut it in two from north to south, and a part or even a greater part of our territory will have fallen into the hands of the enemy and become his rear. We shall have to extend guerrilla warfare all over this vast enemy-occupied area, make a front out of the enemy's rear, and force him to fight ceaselessly throughout the territory he occupies. Until such time as our strategic counter-offensive is launched and so long as our lost territories are not recovered, it will be necessary to persist in guerrilla warfare in the enemy's rear, certainly for a fairly long time, though one cannot say definitely for how long. This is why the war will be a protracted one. And in order to safeguard his gains in the occupied areas, the enemy is bound to step up his anti-guerrilla measures and, especially after the halting of his strategic offensive, to embark on relentless suppression of the guerrillas. With ruthlessness thus added to protractedness, it will be impossible to sustain guerrilla warfare behind the enemy lines without base areas.

What, then, are these base areas? They are the strategic bases on which the guerrilla forces rely in performing their strategic tasks and achieving the object of preserving and expanding themselves and destroying and driving out the enemy. Without such strategic bases, there will be nothing to depend on in carrying out any of our strategic tasks or achieving the aim of the war. It is a characteristic of guerrilla warfare behind the enemy lines that it is fought without a rear, for the guerrilla forces are severed from the country's general rear. But guerrilla warfare could not last long or grow without base areas. The base areas, indeed, are its rear.

History knows many peasant wars of the "roving rebel" type, but none of them ever succeeded. In the present age of advanced communications and technology, it would be all the more groundless to imagine that one can win victory by fighting in the manner of roving rebels. However, this roving-rebel idea still exists among impoverished peasants, and in the minds of guerrilla commanders it becomes the view that base areas are neither necessary nor important. Therefore, ridding the minds of guerrilla commanders of this idea is a prerequisite for deciding on a policy of establishing base areas. The question of whether or not to have base areas and of whether or not to regard them as important, in other words, the conflict between the idea of establishing base areas and that of fighting like roving rebels, arises in all guerrilla warfare, and, to a certain extent, our anti-Japanese guerrilla warfare is no exception. Therefore the struggle against the roving-rebel ideology is an inevitable process. Only when this ideology is thoroughly overcome and the policy of establishing base areas is initiated and applied will there be conditions favorable for the maintenance of guerrilla warfare over a long period.

Now that the necessity and importance of base areas have been made clear, let us pass on to the following problems which must be understood and solved when it comes to establishing the base areas. These problems are the types of base areas, the guerrilla zones and the base areas, the conditions for establishing base areas, their consolidation and expansion, and the forms in which we and the enemy encircle one another.

1. THE TYPES OF BASE AREAS

Base areas in anti-Japanese guerrilla warfare are mainly of three types, those in the mountains, those on the plains and those in the river-lake-estuary regions.

The advantage of setting up base areas in mountainous regions is obvious, and those which have been, are being or will be established in the Changpai,[1] Wutai,[2] Taihang,[3] Taishan,[4] Yenshan [5] and Maoshan [6] Mountains all belong to this type. They are all places where anti-Japanese guerrilla warfare can be maintained for the longest time and are important strongholds for the War of Resistance. We must develop guerrilla warfare and set up base areas in all the mountainous regions behind the enemy lines.

Of course, the plains are less suitable than the mountains, but it is by no means impossible to develop guerrilla warfare or establish any base areas there. Indeed, the widespread guerrilla warfare in the plains of Hopei and of northern and northwestern Shantung proves that it is possible to develop guerrilla warfare in the plains. While there is as yet no evidence on the possibility of setting up base areas there and maintaining them for long, it has been proved that the setting up of temporary base areas is possible, and it should be possible to set up base areas for small units or for seasonal use. On the one hand, the enemy does not have enough troops at his disposal and is pursuing a policy of unparalleled brutality, and on the other hand, China has a vast territory and vast numbers of people who are resisting Japan; the objective conditions for spreading guerrilla warfare and setting up temporary base areas in the plains are therefore fulfilled. Given competent military command, it should of course be possible to establish bases for small guerrilla units there, bases which are long-term but not fixed.[7] Broadly speaking, when the strategic offensive of the enemy is brought to a halt and he enters the stage of safeguarding his occupied areas, he will undoubtedly launch savage attacks on all the guerrilla base areas, and those in the plains will naturally be the first to bear the brunt. The large guerrilla formations operating on the plains will be unable to keep on fighting there for long and will gradually have to move up into the mountains as the circumstances require, as for instance, from the Hopei Plain to the Wutai and Taihang Mountains, or from the Shantung Plain to Taishan Mountain and the Shantung Peninsula in the east. But in the circumstances of our national war it is not impossible for numerous small guerrilla units to keep going in various counties over the vast plains and adopt a fluid way of fighting, i.e., by shifting their bases from place to place. It is definitely possible to conduct seasonal guerrilla warfare by taking advantage of the "green curtain" of tall crops in summer and of the frozen rivers in winter. As the enemy has no strength to spare now and will never be able to attend to everything even when he has the strength to spare, it is absolutely necessary for us to decide on the policy, for the present, of spreading guerrilla warfare far and wide and setting up temporary base areas in the plains and, for the future, of preparing to keep up guerrilla warfare by small units, if only seasonally, and of creating base areas which are not fixed.

Objectively speaking, the possibilities of developing guerrilla warfare and establishing base areas are greater in the river-lake-estuary regions than in the plains, though less than in the mountains. The dramatic battles fought by "pirates" and "water-bandits", of which our history is full, and the guerrilla warfare round the Hunghu Lake kept up for several years in the Red Army period, both testify to the possibility of developing

Mao Zedong

guerrilla warfare and of establishing base areas in the river-lake-estuary regions. So far, however, the political parties and the masses who are resisting Japan have given this possibility little attention. Though the subjective conditions are as yet lacking, we should undoubtedly turn our attention to this possibility and start working on it. As one aspect in the development of our nation-wide guerrilla warfare, we should effectively organize guerrilla warfare in the Hungtse Lake region north of the Yangtse River, in the Taihu Lake region south of the Yangtse, and in all river-lake-estuary regions in the enemy-occupied areas along the rivers and on the seacoast, and we should create permanent base areas in and near such places. By overlooking this aspect we are virtually providing the enemy with water transport facilities; this is a gap in our strategic plan for the War of Resistance which must be filled in good time.

2. GUERRILLA ZONES AND BASE AREAS

In guerrilla warfare behind the enemy lines, there is a difference between guerrilla zones and base areas. Areas which are surrounded by the enemy but whose central parts are not occupied or have been recovered, like some counties in the Wutai mountain region (i.e., the Shansi-Chahar-Hopei border area) and also some places in the Taihang and Taishan mountain regions, are ready-made bases for the convenient use of guerrilla units in developing guerrilla warfare. But elsewhere in these areas the situation is different, as for instance in the eastern and northern sections of the Wutai mountain region, which include parts of western Hopei and southern Chahar, and in many places east of Paoting and west of Tsangchow. When guerrilla warfare began, the guerrillas could not completely occupy these places but could only make frequent raids; they are areas which are held by the guerrillas when they are there and by the puppet regime when they are gone, and are therefore not yet guerrilla bases but only what may be called guerrilla zones. Such guerrilla zones will be transformed into base areas when they have gone through the necessary processes of guerrilla warfare, that is, when large numbers of enemy troops have been annihilated or defeated there, the puppet regime has been destroyed, the masses have been roused to activity, anti-Japanese mass organizations have been formed, people's local armed forces have been developed, and anti-Japanese political power has been established. By the expansion of our base areas we mean the addition of areas such as these to the bases already established.

In some places, for example, eastern Hopei, the whole area of guerrilla operations has been a guerrilla zone from the very beginning. The puppet regime is of long standing there, and from the beginning the whole area of operations has been a guerrilla zone both for the people's armed forces that have grown out of local uprisings and for the guerrilla detachments dispatched from the Wutai Mountains. At the outset of their activities, all they could do was to choose some fairly good spots there as temporary rear or base areas. Such places will not be transformed from guerrilla zones into relatively stable base areas until the enemy forces are destroyed and the work of arousing the people is in full swing.

Thus the transformation of a guerrilla zone into a base area is an arduous creative process, and its accomplishment depends on the extent to which the enemy is destroyed and the masses are aroused.

Many regions will remain guerrilla zones for a long time. In these regions the enemy will not be able to set up stable puppet regimes, however much he tries to maintain control, while we, on our part, will not be able to achieve the aim of establishing anti-Japanese political power, however much we develop guerrilla warfare. Examples of this kind are to be found in the enemy-occupied regions along the railway lines, in the neighborhood of big cities and in certain areas in the plains.

As for the big cities, the railway stops and the areas in the plains which are strongly garrisoned by the enemy, guerrilla warfare can only extend to the fringes and not right into these places which have relatively stable puppet regimes. This is another kind of situation.

Mistakes in our leadership or strong enemy pressure may cause a reversal of the state of affairs described above, i.e., a guerrilla base may turn into a guerrilla zone, and a guerrilla zone may turn into an area under relatively stable enemy occupation. Such changes are possible, and they deserve special vigilance on the part of guerrilla commanders.

Therefore, as a result of guerrilla warfare and the struggle between us and the enemy, the entire enemy-occupied territory will fall into the following three categories: first, anti-Japanese bases held by our guerrilla units and our organs of political power; second, areas held by Japanese imperialism and its puppet regimes; and third, intermediate zones contested by both sides, namely, guerrilla zones. Guerrilla commanders have the duty to expand the first and third categories to the maximum and to reduce the second category to the minimum. This is the strategic task of guerrilla warfare.

3. CONDITIONS FOR ESTABLISHING BASE AREAS

The fundamental conditions for establishing a base area are that there should be anti-Japanese armed forces, that these armed forces should be employed to inflict defeats on the enemy and that they should arouse the people to action. Thus the establishment of a base area is first and foremost a matter of building an armed force. Leaders in guerrilla war must devote their energy to building one or more guerrilla units, and must gradually develop them in the course of struggle into guerrilla formations or even into units and formations of regular troops. The building up of an armed force is the key to establishing a base area; if there is no armed force or if the armed force is weak, nothing can be done. This constitutes the first condition.

The second indispensable condition for establishing a base area is that the armed forces should be used in co-ordination with the people to defeat the enemy. All places under enemy control are enemy, and not guerrilla, base areas, and obviously cannot be transformed into guerrilla base areas unless the enemy is defeated. Unless we repulse the enemy's attacks and defeat him, even places held by the guerrillas will come under enemy control, and then it will be impossible to establish base areas.

The third indispensable condition for establishing a base area is the use of all our strength, including our armed forces, to arouse the masses for struggle against Japan. In the course of this struggle we must arm the people, i.e., organize self-defense corps and guerrilla units. In the course of this struggle, we must form mass organizations, we must organize the workers, peasants, youth, women, children, merchants and professional people -- according to the degree of their political consciousness and fighting enthusiasm -- into the various mass organizations necessary for the struggle against Japanese aggression, and we must gradually expand them. Without organization, the people cannot give effect to their anti-Japanese strength. In the course of this struggle, we must weed out the open and the hidden traitors a task which can be accomplished only by relying on the strength of the people. In this struggle, it is particularly important to arouse the people to establish, or to consolidate, their local organs of anti-Japanese political power. Where the original Chinese organs of political power have not been destroyed by the enemy, we must re-organize and strengthen them with the support of the broad masses, and where they have been destroyed by the enemy, we should rebuild them by the efforts of the masses. They are organs of political power for carrying out the policy of the Anti-Japanese National United Front and should unite all the forces of the people to fight against our sole enemy, Japanese imperialism, and its jackals, the traitors and reactionaries.

A base area for guerrilla war can be truly established only with the gradual fulfillment of the three basic conditions, i.e., only after the anti-Japanese armed forces are built up, the enemy has suffered defeats and the people are aroused.

Mention must also be made of geographical and economic conditions. As for the former, we have already discussed three different categories in the earlier section on the types of base areas, and here we need only mention one major requirement, namely, that the area must be extensive. In places surrounded by the enemy on all sides, or on three sides, the mountainous regions naturally offer the best conditions for setting up base areas which can hold out for a long time, but the main thing is that there must be enough room for the guerrillas to maneuver, namely, the areas have to be extensive. Given an extensive area, guerrilla warfare can be developed and sustained even in the plains, not to mention the river-lake-estuary regions. By and large, the vastness of China's territory and the enemy's shortage of troops provide guerrilla warfare in China with this condition. This is an important, even a primary condition, as far as the possibility of waging guerrilla warfare is concerned, and small countries like Belgium which lack this condition have few or no such possibilities.[8] In China, this condition is not something which has to be striven for, nor does it present a problem; it is there physically, waiting only to be exploited.

So far as their physical setting is concerned, the economic conditions resemble the geographical conditions. For now we are discussing the establishment of base areas not in a desert, where no enemy is to be found, but behind the enemy lines; every place the enemy can penetrate already has its Chinese inhabitants and an economic basis for subsistence, so that the question of choice of economic conditions in establishing base areas simply does not arise. Irrespective of the economic conditions, we should do our utmost to develop guerrilla warfare and set up permanent or temporary base areas in all places where Chinese inhabitants and enemy forces are to be found. In a political sense, however, the economic conditions do present a problem, a problem of economic policy which is of immense importance to the establishment of base areas. The economic policy of the guerrilla base areas must follow the principles of the Anti-Japanese National United Front by equitably distributing the financial burden and protecting commerce. Neither the local organs of political power nor the guerrilla units must violate these principles, or otherwise the establishment of base areas and the maintenance of guerrilla warfare would be adversely affected. The equitable distribution of the financial burden means that "those with money should contribute money", while the peasants should supply the guerrilla units with grain within certain limits. The protection of commerce means that the guerrilla units should be highly disciplined and that the confiscation of shops, except those owned by proved traitors, should be strictly prohibited. This is no easy matter, but the policy is set and must be put into effect.

Mao Zedong

4. THE CONSOLIDATION AND EXPANSION OF BASE AREAS

In order to confine the enemy invaders to a few strongholds, that is, to the big cities and along the main communication lines, the guerrillas must do all they can to extend guerrilla warfare from their base areas as widely as possible and hem in all the enemy's strongholds, thus threatening his existence and shaking his morale while expanding the base areas. This is essential. In this context, we must oppose conservatism in guerrilla warfare. Whether originating in the desire for an easy life or in overestimation of the enemy's strength, conservatism can only bring losses in the War of Resistance and is harmful to guerrilla warfare and to the base areas themselves. At the same time, we must not forget the consolidation of the base areas, the chief task being to arouse and organize the masses and to train guerrilla units and local armed forces. Such consolidation is needed for maintaining protracted warfare and also for expansion, and in its absence energetic expansion is impossible. If we attend only to expansion and forget about consolidation in our guerrilla warfare, we shall be unable to withstand the enemy's attacks, and consequently not only forfeit the possibility of expansion but also endanger the very existence of the base areas. The correct principle is expansion with consolidation, which is a good method and allows us to take the offensive or the defensive as we choose. Given a protracted war, the problem of consolidating and expanding base areas constantly arises for every guerrilla unit. The concrete solution depends, of course, on the circumstances. At one time, the emphasis may be on expansion, i.e., on expanding the guerrilla zones and increasing the number of guerrillas. At another, the emphasis may be on consolidation, i.e., on organizing the masses and training the troops. As expansion and consolidation differ in nature, and as the military dispositions and other tasks will differ accordingly, an effective solution of the problem is possible only if we alternate the emphasis according to time and circumstances.

5. FORMS IN WHICH WE AND THE ENEMY ENCIRCLE ONE ANOTHER

Taking the War of Resistance as a whole, there is no doubt that we are strategically encircled by the enemy, because he is on the strategic offensive and is operating on exterior lines while we are on the strategic defensive and are operating on interior lines. This is the first form of enemy encirclement. We on our part encircle each of the enemy columns advancing on us along separate routes, because we apply the policy of the offensive and of exterior-line operations in campaigns and battles by using numerically preponderant forces against these enemy columns advancing on us from exterior lines. This is the first form of our encirclement of the enemy. Next, if we consider the guerrilla base areas in the enemy's rear, each area taken singly is surrounded by the enemy on all sides, like the Wutai mountain region, or on three sides, like the northwestern Shansi area. This is the second form of enemy encirclement. However, if one considers all the guerrilla base areas together and in their relation to the battle fronts of the regular forces, one can see that we in turn surround a great many enemy forces. In Shansi Province, for instance, we have surrounded the Tatung-Puchow Railway on three sides (the east and west flanks and the southern end) and the city of Taiyuan on all sides; and there are many similar instances in Hopei and Shantung Provinces. This is the second form of our encirclement of the enemy. Thus there are two forms of encirclement by the enemy forces and two forms of encirclement by our own -- rather like a game of weichi.[9] Campaigns and battles fought by the two sides resemble the capturing of each other's pieces, and the establishment of strongholds by the enemy and of guerrilla base areas by us resembles moves to dominate spaces on the board. It is in the matter of "dominating the spaces" that the great strategic role of guerrilla base areas in the rear of the enemy is revealed.

We are raising this question in the War of Resistance in order that the nation's military authorities and the guerrilla commanders in all areas should place on the agenda the development of guerrilla warfare behind the enemy lines and the establishment of base areas wherever possible, and carry this out as a strategic task. If on the international plane we can create an anti-Japanese front in the Pacific region, with China as one strategic unit, and the Soviet Union and other countries which may join it as other strategic units, we shall then have one more form of encirclement against the enemy than he has against us and bring about exterior-line operations in the Pacific region by which to encircle and destroy fascist Japan.

To be sure, this is of little practical significance at present, but such a prospect is not impossible.

Chapter 7

The Strategic Defensive and the Strategic Offensive in Guerrilla War

The fourth problem of strategy in guerrilla war concerns the strategic defensive and the strategic offensive. This is the problem of how the policy of offensive warfare, which we mentioned in our discussion of the first problem, is to be carried out in practice, when we are on the defensive and when we are on the offensive in our guerrilla warfare against Japan.

Within the nation-wide strategic defensive or strategic offensive (to be more exact, the strategic counter-offensive), small-scale strategic defensives and offensives take place in and around each guerrilla base area. By strategic defensive we mean our strategic situation and policy when the enemy is on the offensive and we are on the defensive; by strategic offensive we mean our strategic situation and policy when the enemy is on the defensive and we are on the offensive.

1. THE STRATEGIC DEFENSIVE IN GUERRILLA WAR

After guerrilla warfare has broken out and grown to a considerable extent, the enemy will inevitably attack the guerrilla base areas, especially in the period when his strategic offensive against the country as a whole is brought to an end and he adopts the policy of safeguarding his occupied areas. It is essential to recognize the inevitability of such attacks, for otherwise the guerrilla commanders will be caught wholly unprepared, and in the face of heavy enemy attacks they will undoubtedly become alarmed and confused and their forces will be routed.

To wipe out the guerrillas and their base areas, the enemy frequently resorts to converging attacks. For instance, in each of the four or five "punitive expeditions" directed against the Wutai mountain region, the enemy made a planned advance in three, four or even six or seven columns simultaneously. The larger the scale of the guerrilla fighting, the more important the position of the base areas, and the greater the threat to the enemy's strategic centers and vital communication lines, the fiercer will be the enemy's attacks. Therefore, the fiercer the enemy's attacks on a guerrilla area, the greater the indication that the guerrilla warfare there is successful and is being effectively co-ordinated with the regular fighting.

When the enemy launches a converging attack in several columns, the guerrilla policy should be to smash it by counter-attack. It can be easily smashed if each advancing enemy column consists of only one unit, whether big or small, has no follow-up units and is unable to station troops along the route of advance, construct blockhouses or build motor roads. When the enemy launches a converging attack, he is on the offensive and operating on exterior lines, while we are on the defensive and operating on interior lines. As for our dispositions, we should use our secondary forces to pin down several enemy columns, while our main force should launch surprise attacks (chiefly in the form of ambushes) in a campaign or battle against a single enemy column, striking it when it is on the move. The enemy, though strong, will be weakened by repeated surprise attacks and will often withdraw when he is halfway; the guerrilla units can then make more surprise attacks during the pursuit and weaken him still further. The enemy generally occupies the county towns or other towns in our base areas before he stops his offensive or begins to withdraw, and we should encircle these towns, cutting off his grain supply and severing his communications, so that when he cannot hold out and begins to retreat, we can seize the opportunity to pursue and attack him. After smashing one column, we should shift our forces to smash another, and, by smashing them one by one, shatter the converging attack.

A big base area like the Wutai mountain region forms a military area, which is divided into four or five, or even more, military sub-areas, each with its own armed forces operating independently. By employing the tactics described above, these forces have often smashed the enemy's attacks simultaneously or successively.

In our plan of operations against a converging attack by the enemy, we generally place our main force on interior lines. But when we have the strength to spare, we should use our secondary forces (such as the county or the district guerrilla units, or even detachments of the main force) on exterior lines to disrupt the enemy's communications and pin down his reinforcements. Should the enemy stay put in our base area, we may reverse the tactics, namely, leave some of our forces in the base area to invest the enemy while employing the main force to attack the region whence he has come and to step up our activities there, in order to induce him to withdraw and attack our main force; this is the tactic of "relieving the state of Chao by besieging the state of Wei".[10]

In the course of operations against a converging attack, the local anti-Japanese self-defense corps and all the mass organizations should mobilize for action and in every way help our troops to fight the enemy. In fighting the enemy, it is important both to enforce local martial law and, as far as possible, to "strengthen our defense works and clear the fields". The purpose of the former is to suppress traitors and prevent the enemy from getting information, and of the latter to assist our own operations (by strengthening our defense works) and prevent the enemy from getting food (by clearing the fields). "Clearing the fields" means harvesting the crops as soon as they are ripe.

When the enemy retreats, he often burns down the houses in the cities and towns he has occupied and razes the villages along his route, with the purpose of destroying the guerrilla base areas; but in so doing he deprives himself of shelter and food in his next offensive, and the damage recoils upon his own head. This is a concrete illustration of what we mean by one and the same thing having two contradictory aspects.

A guerrilla commander should not think of abandoning his base area and shifting to another, unless it proves impossible, after repeated operations, to smash the enemy's heavy converging attacks. In these circumstances he must guard against pessimism. So long as the leaders do not blunder in matters of principle, it is generally possible to smash the converging attacks and hold on to the base areas in the mountainous regions. It is only in the plains that, when confronted by a heavy converging attack, the guerrilla commander should consider other measures in the light of the specific circumstances, namely, leaving many small units for scattered operations, while temporarily shifting large guerrilla formations to some mountainous region, so that they can return and resume their activities in the plains once the main forces of the enemy move away.

Generally speaking, the Japanese cannot adopt the principle of blockhouse warfare, which the Kuomintang employed in the days of the civil war, because their forces are inadequate in relation to China's vast territory. However, we should reckon with the possibility that they may use it to some extent against those guerrilla base areas which pose a particular threat to their vital positions, but even in such circumstances we should be prepared to keep up guerrilla warfare n those areas. Since we have had the experience of being able to maintain guerrilla warfare during the civil war, there is not the slightest doubt of our greater capacity to do so in a national war. Though, in point of relative military strength, the enemy can throw forces that are vastly superior in quantity as well as in quality against some of our base areas, there remain the insoluble national contradiction between us and the enemy and the unavoidable weaknesses of his command. Our victories are based on thorough work among the masses and flexible tactics in our operations.

2. THE STRATEGIC OFFENSIVE IN GUERRILLA WAR

After we have smashed an enemy offensive and before the enemy starts a new offensive, he is on the strategic defensive and we are on the strategic offensive.

At such times our operational policy is not to attack enemy forces which are entrenched in defensive positions and which we are not sure of defeating, but systematically to destroy or drive out the small enemy units and puppet forces in certain areas, which our guerrilla units are strong enough to deal with, and to expand our areas, arouse the masses for struggle against Japan, replenish and train our troops and organize new guerrilla units. If the enemy still remains on the defensive when these tasks are under way, we can expand our new areas still further and attack weakly garrisoned cities and communication lines and hold them for as long as circumstances permit. These are all tasks of the strategic offensive, and the purpose is to take advantage of the fact that the enemy is on the defensive so that we may effectively build up our own military and mass strength, effectively reduce the enemy's strength and prepare to smash the enemy methodically and vigorously when he mounts an offensive again.

It is essential to rest and train our troops, and the best time for doing so is when the enemy is on the defensive. It is not a question of shutting ourselves off from everything else for rest and training, but of finding time for rest and training while expanding our areas, mopping up small enemy units and arousing the people. This is usually also the time for tackling the difficult problem of getting food supplies, bedding, clothing, etc.

It is also the time for destroying the enemy's communication lines on a large scale, hampering his transport and giving direct support to the regular forces in their campaigns.

At such times the guerrilla base areas, guerrilla zones and guerrilla units are in high spirits, and the areas devastated by the enemy are gradually rehabilitated and revived. The people in the enemy-occupied territories are also delighted, and the fame of the guerrillas resounds everywhere. On the other hand, in the camp of the enemy and his running dogs, the traitors, panic and disintegration are mounting, while there is growing hatred of the guerrillas and their base areas and preparations to deal with them are intensified. During the strategic offensive, therefore, it is impermissible for the guerrilla commanders to become so elated as to underrate the enemy and forget to strengthen unity in their own ranks and to consolidate their base areas and their forces. At such times, they must skillfully watch the enemy's every move for signs of any new offensive against us, so that the moment it comes they can wind up their strategic offensive in good order, turn to the strategic defensive and thereby smash the enemy's offensive.

Chapter 8

Development of Guerrilla War into Mobile War

The fifth problem of strategy in guerrilla war against Japan is its development into mobile war, a development which is necessary and possible because the war is protracted and ruthless. If China could speedily defeat the Japanese invaders and recover her lost territories, and if the war were neither protracted nor ruthless, this would not be necessary. But as, on the contrary, the war is protracted and ruthless, guerrilla warfare cannot adapt itself to such a war except by developing into mobile warfare. Since the war is protracted and ruthless, it is possible for the guerrilla units to undergo the necessary steeling and gradually to transform themselves into regular forces, so that their mode of operations is gradually regularized and guerrilla warfare develops into mobile warfare. The necessity and possibility of this development must be clearly recognized by the guerrilla commanders if they are to persist in, and systematically carry out, the policy of turning guerrilla warfare into mobile warfare.

In many places, such as the Wutai mountain region, the present guerrilla warfare owes its growth to the strong detachments sent there by the regular forces. The operations there, though generally of a guerrilla character, have contained an element of mobile warfare from the very beginning. This element will gradually increase as the war goes on. Herein lies the advantage which makes possible the swift expansion of the present anti-Japanese guerrilla warfare and its rapid development to a higher level; thus the conditions for guerrilla warfare are far superior to what they were in the three northeastern provinces.

To transform guerrilla units waging guerrilla warfare into regular forces waging mobile warfare, two conditions are necessary -- an increase in numbers, and an improvement in quality. Apart from directly mobilizing the people to join the forces, increased numbers can be attained by amalgamating small units, while better quality depends on steeling the fighters and improving their weapons in the course of the war.

In amalgamating small units, we must, on the one hand, guard against localism, whereby attention is concentrated exclusively on local interests and centralization is impeded, and, on the other, guard against the purely military approach, whereby local interests are brushed aside.

Localism exists among the local guerrilla units and local governments, which are frequently preoccupied with local considerations to the neglect of the general interest, or which prefer to act each on its own because they are unaccustomed to acting in larger groups. The commanders of the main guerrilla units or of the guerrilla formations must take this into account and adopt the method of gradual amalgamation of part of the local units, allowing the localities to keep some of their forces and expand their guerrilla warfare; the commanders should draw these units into joint operations and then bring about their amalgamation without breaking up their original organization or reshuffling their cadres, so that the small groups may integrate smoothly into the larger group.

As against localism, the purely military approach represents the wrong viewpoint held in the main forces by those who are bent on expanding their own strength and who neglect to assist the local armed units. They do not realize that the development of guerrilla warfare into mobile warfare means not the abandonment of guerrilla warfare, but the gradual formation, in the midst of widespread guerrilla warfare, of a main force capable of conducting mobile warfare, a force around which there must still be numerous guerrilla units carrying on extensive guerrilla operations. These guerrilla units are powerful auxiliaries to the main force and serve as inexhaustible reserves for its continuous growth. Therefore, if a commander of a main force has made the mistake of neglecting the interests of the local population and the local government as a result of a purely military approach, he must correct it in order that the expansion of the main force and the multiplication of the local armed units may both receive due attention.

To raise the quality of the guerrilla units it is imperative to raise their political and organizational level and improve their equipment, military technique, tactics and discipline, so that they gradually pattern themselves on the regular forces and shed their guerrilla ways. Politically, it is imperative to get both the commanders and the fighters to realize the necessity of raising the guerrilla units to the level of the regular forces, to encourage them to strive towards this end, and to guarantee its attainment by means of political work. Organizationally, it is imperative gradually to fulfill all the requirements of a regular formation in the following respects -- military and political organs, staff and working methods, a regular supply system, a medical service, etc. In the matter of equipment, it is imperative to acquire: better and more varied weapons and increase the supply of the necessary communications equipment. In the matter of military technique and tactics, it is imperative to raise the guerrilla units to the level required of a regular formation. In the matter of discipline, it is imperative to raise the level so that uniform standards are observed, every order is executed without fail and all slackness is eliminated. To accomplish all these tasks requires a prolonged effort, and it cannot be done overnight; but that is the direction in which we must develop. Only thus can a main force be built up in each guerrilla base area and mobile warfare emerge for more effective attacks on the enemy. Where detachments or cadres have been sent in by the regular forces, the goal can be achieved more easily. Hence all the regular forces have the responsibility of helping the guerrilla units to develop into regular units.

Chapter 9

The Relationship of Command

The last problem of strategy in guerrilla war against Japan concerns the relationship of command. A correct solution of this problem is one of the prerequisites for the unhampered development of guerrilla warfare.

Since guerrilla units are a lower level of armed organization characterized by dispersed operations, the methods of command in guerrilla warfare do not allow as high a degree of centralization as in regular warfare. If any attempt is made to apply the methods of command in regular warfare to guerrilla warfare, its great flexibility will inevitably be restricted and its vitality sapped. A highly centralized command is in direct contradiction to the great flexibility of guerrilla warfare and must not and cannot be applied to it.

However, guerrilla warfare cannot be successfully developed without some centralized command. When extensive regular warfare and extensive guerrilla warfare are going on at the same time, their operations must be properly co-ordinated; hence the need for a command co-ordinating the two, i.e., for a unified strategic command by the national general staff and the war-zone commanders. In a guerrilla zone or guerrilla base area with many guerrilla units, there are usually one or more guerrilla formations (sometimes together with regular formations) which constitute the main force, a number of other guerrilla units, big and small, which represent the supplementary force, and many armed units composed of people not withdrawn from production; the enemy forces there usually form a unified complex to concert their operations against the guerrillas. Consequently, the problem arises of setting up a unified or centralized command in such guerrilla zones or base areas.

Hence, as opposed both to absolute centralization and to absolute decentralization, the principle of command in guerrilla war should be centralized strategic command and decentralized command in campaigns and battles.

Centralized strategic command includes the planning and direction of guerrilla warfare as a whole by the state, the coordination of guerrilla warfare with regular warfare in each war zone, and the unified direction of all the anti-Japanese armed forces in each guerrilla zone or base area. Here lack of harmony, unity and centralization is harmful, and every effort must be made to ensure all three. In general matters, that is, matters of strategy, the lower levels should report to the higher and follow their instructions so as to ensure concerted action. Centralization, however, stops at this point, and it would likewise be harmful to go beyond it and interfere with the lower levels in matters of detail like the specific dispositions for a campaign or battle. For such details must be settled in the light of specific conditions, which change from time to time and from place to place and are quite beyond the knowledge of the distant higher levels of command. This is what is meant by the principle of decentralized command in campaigns and battles. The same principle generally applies in regular operations, especially when communications are inadequate. In a word, it means guerrilla warfare waged independently and with the initiative in our hands within the framework of a unified strategy.

Where a guerrilla base area constitutes a military area divided into sub-areas, each comprising several counties, each of which is again divided into districts, the relationship between the various levels, from the headquarters of the military area and sub-areas down to the county and district governments, is one of consecutive subordination, and every armed force must, according to its nature, be under the direct command of one of these. On the principle that has been enunciated, in the relationship of command at these levels matters of general policy should be centralized in the higher levels, while actual operations should be carried out in the light of the specific circumstances by the lower levels, which should have the right of independent action. If a higher level has something to say about the actual operations undertaken at a lower level, it can and should advance its views as "instructions" but must not issue hard and fast "commands". The more extensive the area, the more complex the situation and the greater the distance between the higher and the lower levels, the more advisable it becomes to allow greater independence to the lower levels in their actual operations and thus give those operations a character conforming more closely to the local requirements, so that the lower levels and the local personnel may develop the ability to work independently, cope with complicated situations, and successfully expand guerrilla warfare. For an armed unit or bigger formation which is engaged in a concentrated operation, the principle to be applied is one of centralization in its internal relationship of command, since the situation is clear to the higher command but the moment this unit or formation breaks up for dispersed action, the principle of centralization in general matters and of decentralization in details should be applied, for then the specific situation cannot be clear to the higher command. Absence of centralization where it is needed means negligence by the higher levels or usurpation of authority by the lower levels, neither of which can be tolerated in the relationship between higher and lower levels, especially in the military sphere. If decentralization is not effected where it should be, that means monopolization of power by the higher levels and lack of initiative on the part of the lower levels, neither of which can be tolerated in the relationship between higher and lower levels, especially in the command of guerrilla war fare. The above principles constitute the only correct policy for solving the problem of the relationship of command.

NOTES

[1] The Changpai mountain range is situated on the northeastern border of China. After the Japanese invasion on September 18, 1931, the region became a base area for the anti-Japanese guerrillas led by the Chinese Communist Party.

[2] The Wutai mountain range is situated on the borders between Shansi, Hopei and what was then Chahar Province. In October 1937 the Eighth Route Army led by the Chinese Communist Party started building the Shansi-Chahar-Hopei anti-Japanese base area with the Wutai mountain region as its centre.

[3] The Taihang mountain range is situated on the borders between Shansi, Hopei and Honan Provinces. In November 1937 the Eighth Route Army started building the southeastern Shansi anti-Japanese base area with the Taihang mountain region as its centre.

[4] The Taishan Mountain is one of the chief peaks of the Tai-Yi mountain range in central Shantung. In the winter of 1937 the guerrilla forces led by the Communist Party started building the central Shantung anti-Japanese base area with the Tai-Yi mountain region as its centre.

[5] The Yenshan mountain range is situated on the border of Hopei and what was then Jehol Province. In the summer of 1938 the Eighth Route Army started building the eastern Hopei anti-Japanese base area with the Yenshan mountain region as its centre.

[6] The Maoshan Mountains are in southern Kiangsu. In June 1938 the New Fourth Army led by the Communist Party

Mao Zedong

started building the southern Kiangsu anti-Japanese base area with the Maoshan mountain region as its centre.

[7] Experience gained in the War of Resistance proved that it was possible to establish long-term and, in many places, stable base areas in the plains. This was due to their vastness and big populations, the correctness of the Communist Party's policies, the extensive mobilization of the people and the enemy's shortage of troops. Comrade Mao Zedong affirmed this possibility more definitely in later directives.

[8] Ever since the end of World War II, the national and democratic revolutionary movement has been surging forward in Asia, Africa and Latin America. In many countries the people, led by their own revolutionary and progressive forces, have carried on sustained armed struggles to overthrow the dark rule of imperialism and reaction. This demonstrates that in the new historical circumstances -- when the socialist camp, the revolutionary forces of the people in the colonial countries and the forces of the people striving for democracy and progress in all countries are taking giant strides forward, when the world capitalist system is weakening still further, and when the colonial rule of imperialism is heading for disintegration -- the conditions under which the people of various countries conduct guerrilla warfare today need not be quite the same as those which were necessary in the days of the guerrilla warfare waged by the Chinese people against Japan. In other words, guerrilla war can be victoriously waged in a country which is not large in territory, as for instance, in Cuba, Algeria, Laos and southern Viet Nam.

[9] Weichi is an old Chinese game, in which the two players try to encircle each other's pieces on the board. When a player's pieces are encircled, they are counted as "dead" (captured). But

if there is a sufficient number of blank spaces among the encircled pieces, then the latter are still "alive" (not captured).

[10] In 353 B.C. the state of Wei laid siege to Hantan, capital of the state of Chao. The king of the state of Chi, an ally of Chao, ordered his generals Tien Chi and Sun Pin to aid Chao with their troops. Knowing that the crack forces of Wei had entered Chao and left their own territory weakly garrisoned, General Sun Pin attacked the state of Wei whose troops withdrew to defend their own country. Taking advantage of their exhaustion, the troops of Chi engaged and routed them at Kueiling (northeast of the present Hotse County in Shantung). The siege of Hantan, capital of Chao, was thus lifted. Since then Chinese strategists have referred to similar tactics as "relieving the state of Chao by besieging the state of Wei".

Also Available

The Art of War – Special Edition

- The Art of War by Sun Tzu – Special Edition
- The Art of War by Baron de Jomini – Special Edition
- The Art of War by Mao Tse-tung – Special Edition
- The Art of War & The Prince – Special Edition

Asian Philosophy Collection

- Tao – The Way – Special Edition
- The Teachings of Confucius – Special Edition
- Zen: Religion of the Samurai
- The Samurai Series

Greco-Roman Studies

- Ethics and Politics – Aristotle
- The History of the Peloponnesian War – Thucydides
- Anabasis: The March Up Country – Xenophon
- Caesar's Commentaries – Julius Caesar

Classical Literature

- Beowulf – In Old English & New English
- Siddhartha – In German & English – Herman Hesse
- The Aeneid of Virgil
- The Iliad & The Odyssey - Homer

Available at Amazon,
your local bookstore,
or through our website:

www.elpasonortepress.com

9 781934 255278